WITHOUT A NET
The Female Experience
of Growing Up Working Class

WITHOUT A NET

The Female Experience
of Growing Up Working Class

Edited by Michelle Tea

SEAL PRESS

Without a Net: The Female Experience of Growing Up Working Class

 Published by
Seal Press
An Imprint of Avalon Publishing Group Incorporated
1400 65th Street, Suite 250
Emeryville, CA 94608

Excerpt from "What I Ate Where" by Diane di Prima was originally published in the collection *Dinner and Nightmares*, published by Last Gasp in 1998. Reprinted by permission of the author.

"Steal Away" by Dorothy Allison was originally published in the collection *Trash*, published by Plume in 2002. Reprinted by permission of the author.

ISBN-10: 1-58005-103-0
ISBN-13: 978-1-58005-103-3

Library of Congress Cataloging-in-Publication Data
Without a net: The female experience of growing up working class / [edited] by Michelle Tea.-- 1st ed.
p. cm.
ISBN 1-58005-103-0 (pbk.)
1. Working class women—United States. I. Tea, Michelle.
HD6095.W63 2003
305.48/9623--dc22
2004299040

9 8 7 6 5 4 3

Design by Jacob Goolkasian
Printed in the United States of America by Malloy
Distributed by Publishers Group West

TABLE OF CONTENTS

For Theresa Tomasik

INTRODUCTION

When I was in fifth grade I came upon the book *The Outsiders* and it split my world open. That it was written by both a girl and a poor person was clear to me, because here was a raw and sensitive look at the reality of being poor. In *The Outsiders*, all the protagonists are poor, and there is much tragedy. But the tragedy isn't their poverty, it's what happens to them *because* of their poverty, the way the world judges and despises them, fights and blames them, makes their lives plenty hard. The book displays the joys of being poor, the physicality of fighting, the closeness of being in a gang, the tiny triumph of shoplifting. And in the end, the bad kids don't turn good, turn middle-class. In the end, resolution comes when the main character links his struggle as a "greaser"—a poor kid—to the struggles of all the other poor kids out there, struggling to be understood and to survive, and he decides to tell his story. He writes a book, and the book is *The Outsiders*. Transcendent, it turns in on itself, the book eating its own tail. It made me want to write my own books, and I have. I can feel the influence of S. E. Hinton's Ponyboy on my own words, and in the spirit of the story I want to tell, the story of growing up a girl on the margins of the world, where the poor people are. The particulars of how poverty impacts females—their bodies, their sense of themselves, their options. And how it marks you for your whole life, how even if you decide to pass as a middle-class person in

XII

the world (and manage to pull off such a feat), you're still carrying that poor little child around somewhere inside you, in your heart or your gut, or in your mind, where she has spun herself into fearful notions of scarcity and less-than.

I love to read the stories of the working class. It's my home, and I like to see it represented. It always feels like a tiny bit of justice when a poor person manages to get their stories published. For years I've been going to literary readings and poetry open mics, I've been reading zines and self-published chapbooks, and I've been collecting, in my head, the working-class writers I've heard and read. I've wanted them all in one place, together, in the pages of a book I can selfishly pick up and enjoy whenever I want. I've wanted them all together in a book as another piece of justice, to correct the cultural misunderstanding that poor people don't have voices because they don't have anything to say. The misunderstanding that we're comfortable letting well-meaning middle-class writers speak for us. The misunderstanding that our writing isn't out there because we don't write. So many misunderstandings and so many underestimations! One little book isn't going to create the drastic change in perception that our society needs, but it's something. A united force of fierce truth-telling to entertain, educate, and attempt to even the score.

I was talking recently to a friend of mine, a guy who grew up in the same lousy, disadvantaged city I was raised in. He was talking about the freedom he felt as a working-class teenage boy in that town, how fun it was to run the streets, feeling like you owned the place, swiping hub caps, indulging in petty vandalism, no doubt terrorizing the females they tromped past with their simple presence. He stopped for a minute and said, as if thinking it for the first time, "I guess girls didn't really have the freedom we did, huh?" I wanted to smack him in the head. Um, no, not really. Most poor places are tough and most tough places are violent and in violent places females are easy targets. As tough and wild as poor girls might have looked held up against our better-off sisters, we're probably not as tough or wild as the boys we had to share our neighborhoods with. What's it like to grow up receiving messages from the dominant culture that to be a female is to behave in a way that will get you eaten for lunch in your roughneck city?

What's it like to be viewed as dirty, stupid, or promiscuous simply because you're broke? Where are the females in *The Outsiders?* Even Ponyboy, our bookish, sensitive, only-fights-when-he-has-to narrator disses the greaser girls every chance he gets. The upper-class "Soc" girls are smart and classy; Cherry Valance, the only girl in the book, is a Soc but a greaser ally, a sort of dream girl. No greaser girls speak, they're written off as tough and trashy, wearing too much makeup. Sounds depressingly familiar. I wanted, of course, to know their stories. That being impossible, I collected these first-person narratives by females who grew up poor or working class.

I named this book *Without a Net* because I wanted to capture the breath-taking, exhilarating, and scary experience of going through life knowing that there is no safety net to catch you should you fuck up and fall. There is no trust fund, no parents with cash on hand to cover a month's rent; the way the stress of being poor or working class can rip apart a family or destroy its members often means there's no family to call, period. Sometimes the net you're surviving without is that simple emotional support. I like to imagine that our lives are dazzling athletic feats, our survival graceful and artistic. It's a romantic way of looking at it, but you can't fault me for wanting to highlight our strengths, the brilliant flare of our collective defiance. When poor and working-class people are written about—and usually we are written *about,* rarely telling our own stories— it's always the tragedy that is documented. The incessant struggle, the rampant injustice.

Barbara Ehrenreich's smash bestseller *Nickel and Dimed: On (Not) Getting By in America* is a great example of this: fainting Merry Maids! Overworked, underpaid Wal-Mart workers! I try, I really do, to keep the cynicism and general bad attitude I have toward Ehrenreich's book in check. Truly her intentions were noble—to sink into the world of the minimum-wage worker, emerge with first-hand proof that it is a rough world, an impossible, soul-slaughtering existence. The problem, perhaps, is not her project itself, or even the fact that she was terribly well paid to be poor for a while. Perhaps the reason I found my cracked teeth gritting and my stomach scrambling with frustration while I read is that I couldn't believe this was news, a big hit, a bestseller. *Duh,* I thought, again and again, leafing through the book. Of course minimum-wage work is bone-crushing drudgery, difficult to live on, even more difficult to get out of. Why did it take a middle-class woman on a well-paid slumming vacation to break this news to the world? Where are the voices of the poor people who don't get to leave these lives when the story is completed? The people whose stories generally don't get completed? I knew that these stories were out there, and the image they'd present of the working-class experience in the U.S. would be deeper and more complicated than the tragic view the middle class always takes on our lives. There's tragedy, for sure there's tragedy, but there are also kick-ass survival skills to be proud of, so many ingenious approaches to surviving poverty—everything from the focused, determined march out from under it via college and hard work to a gleeful, defiant, dumpster-diving exultation in the freedom that can accompany living at the bottom. There is joy in poor people's lives, and humor and camaraderie. Girls who grow up working class grow up tough and clever. There is hope in our lives, whether it's the pure potential of a Lotto ticket and a bingo card, or the deep faith that things are gonna get better 'cause they sure as hell can't get any worse. We know the world is vast and complicated, our responses to our situations are often contradictory, counterintuitive, but we get by. We are all survivors, and have no use for the pity and condescension that often accompany discussions about our lives.

Discussions, incidentally, that we're rarely a part of. Poor people are always left out of the intellectual conversation, despite being the subjects of entire books. In *Nickel and Dimed,* Ehrenreich, a successful middle-class woman, speaks directly to other middle-class people. This happens frequently in books and articles about working-class people—it is assumed that none of us will be reading the text. It's a decidedly creepy experience to read about your life like this, passed from one middle-class perception to another. It's like being talked about in a room where you sit, invisible. It's a game of intellectual keep-away, the words lobbed over your head, but worse—no one even knows you're trying to get in on the game. It doesn't even occur to them that you could play.

*   *   *

I'm trying to straighten this all out a bit with the publication of this collection. It's been a frustrating search, looking for writing in which poor women get to tell *their* stories. As far as anthologies go, this may be the only one in print. May it start an enormous trend. Either way, we'll still be writing. We don't write to be fast-tracked into publishing glory—many of us haven't even gone to school, and even those who have still stumble a bit through life. For us, writing isn't a career so much as it is a vocation, a life saver, a way to prove, to ourselves at least, that we actually exist, that our struggles aren't for nothing, that our lives are meaningful, are triumphant. We write to release old injustices and abuses, to make sense of them, to contextualize ourselves. We write to tell the truth, our writings like graffiti on the surface of the moneyed culture at large. We write so that we can finally see our experiences portrayed honestly, in many dimensions. And like all writers, we write because it is simply what we do. But for poor and working-class writers, writing itself is a survival skill.

A note with regard to gender: *Without a Net* aims to capture the experiences of growing up poor and female; submissions were accepted from anyone assigned female at birth and/or at present identifying as female.

Michelle Tea
San Francisco, 2003

WAITING

Maria Rivera

Being poor means waiting, for everything. Today, I'm waiting for meds at County Hospital. Apparently, at age twenty-seven, I am incapable of leaving my house, let alone functioning in society, without being medicated. It used to be I could go to the public health clinic by Cabrini Green and wait two to three hours, the doctor would ask what I wanted and give me a bag full of samples. Now I have to register at County, get a number, and hope. Hope they find me poor enough and crazy enough to need the meds, that they can order them for me, that in a month or so I can come back and pick them up. Thank god it's not a heart condition or I could be dead by then. My day started at 5:30 A.M., when I lined up outside with about sixty of my desperate neighbors who had the foresight to get here early. At about 7 A.M., they let us in. By the time I get to give my spiel to a nurse it's one o'clock in the afternoon and she informs me that if I leave for any reason and miss the doctor calling me, I will have to start at the back of the line. Super, because my bladder is about to go and I now understand why everyone else brought a partner to stay with them all day.

I find a seat when some guy with gold teeth finally gets up to use the vending machine. I am squeezed between a carny and a nanny from Russia. The carny is telling everyone within earshot that he used to go to the vet hospital, but nowadays you have to wait at least two days before you get seen there. He's here for a tooth extraction. Grinning with no shame, he opens up a mouthful of green and yellow rot that smells like raw sewage. I'm wondering if he's getting them all out, and of course he's going to give it up. "Third from the left, been hurtin' like hell all the way since Tampa." Oh, we all nod. I am doing my best not to inhale in his direction, and catch the eye of my other neighbor while taking a big whiff from her side. I open my backpack, filled to the brim with bullshit. I'm a bitch for fashion magazines, and thank god my landlord subscribes to them all and I live in a big building where everyone helps themselves to everyone else's mail. I decide to skip the bottle of water I brought since I won't be able to use a bathroom for the next few hours, and open the big-ass *Vogue* bible of spring. The nanny is breathing so hard down my neck I keep waiting to hear the porn music start over the intercom. She keeps saying things like, "*Oooo*, the tankini, that looks good on any figure," all low and in a really thick accent. After about thirty pages, I turn my head as far as it will go without touching her cheek and mumble, "Why don't you take it." I throw it on her lap. She looks up at me like I am Mother Mary bestowing some great gift and grabs my hands, all glassy-eyed. It's the little things on a day like today, I suppose.

Fortunately, about a third of the poor and desolate women who ended up in Chicago were given the same name as me. I am kept vigilant by the constant stream of Maria's being called up over the speakers. Someone told me that in most heavily Catholic regions the world over, people name their children Maria, as a lifelong blessing and to guarantee that the Virgin Mary will watch out for them. I would like to give a heads-up here and say the numbers just don't seem to be proving this great honor. I turn my attention back to the carny. Now he's chipping some glue off the back of his sweaty, held-together-by-a-thread leather jacket. My lap is covered in what looks like giant-sized dandruff. Last night, at some bar in Ohio, his son wanted his Harley patch. Being the ever-attentive father, the carny ripped it off his jacket and bestowed it upon his much-deserving son. He is now preparing the surface for a newer, better, eagle-wings Harley patch he picked up in Kentucky. He would also like to mention that for a mere thirty-five dollars we can buy passes to ride all the rides at his carnival this weekend. I'm thinkin' if I had thirty-five dollars I'd buy a half a month's prescription of Zoloft and get on with my life. For at least two weeks, anyways. You see, my sanity costs, at minimum, seventy dollars a month. That's without the ten-dollar tyrosine I get at the health food store to actually kick the Zoloft in. If I want to breathe as well—I have the lung capacity of a squirrel—it costs another sixty dollars or so.

The man with the gold teeth whose seat I fell into keeps staring me down from the corner. If I'd had a little more time this morning I would have done my hair and applied my face and I could just look up, smile, and all would be forgiven. As luck would have it, I'm sporting a rat's nest and my natural purplish-yellow complexion, my too-small jeans and a pajama shirt I just can't seem to get away from this week. You never know who will have your fate in their hands when you're applying for any "free" service. Less is more, as they say. It's better to err on the side of "couldn't look more broke"—certainly better than getting rejected because you wore your good clothes and brushed your teeth. One of my high school friends' crack-head mother pointed this out to us when we were applying for free birth control. I think I was fifteen, and it was one of the best survival tips I ever got.

Out of the corner of my eye I am trying to appraise the value of this guy's gold teeth. After many years of pawning anything in my possession worth over five dollars I would guess that, with the top front row alone, I could buy my meds, pay my three-month-old gas bill, and get me and the friend of my choice drunk tonight. Some people just don't know how to manage their money.

By 5 P.M. I am void of any hope. Apparently rotting teeth and crabs— oh yes, crabs, the nanny broke it down—rate much higher than depression, panic, and the inability to breathe. Even the gold teeth are gone. At 6 P.M. I finally hear my name. An angel in a periwinkle smock and a weave that—I could be hallucinating—looks like a small, alien hover-craft is beckoning me from the green door. Green means go, in case you haven't been in County before.

Now it's time for my recital—of my sketchy medical history, that is. Today my audience is an internist, a psychiatrist, two med students, and my trusty nurse. I recount with great post-traumatic stress disorder–style detail two of my favorite and most horrifying medical roller coaster rides. "It all started when I was . . ." is how I like to begin. I open with "The Abortion," a tried-and-true stunner.

I went to get an abortion because my boyfriend refused to wear condoms, and because I hated him and could not bear to think of a whole life biologically tied to him through a little bundle of joy. I went to the budget clinic where for two hundred and fifty dollars I would be free and clear. For another hundred I could be free and clear *and* have general anesthesia. So I guilt-tripped my boyfriend, because really, it was the least he could do. After three hours of education and waiting for them to decide if I was a "good candidate" for an abortion, the budget clinic nurse told me to strip, gown up, and wait in the hall. There was a long line down the hall. Old and young, all different colors of women, and one girl with her mother, who I was so jealous of I could scream.

As we moved down the hallway I could hear the women in front of me getting on a table, and then the countdown till they were numbed out, and, finally, the vacuum. Then they got ushered out the back door on a gurney. Right before me was a girl I totally wanted to be. Rock-star hair, perfect body, super cool, popping her gum the whole time. She went in and they started without anything for pain. She said, "Just stop, let me call someone, I can get the money, *please.*" And then the doctor: "If I stop now, you'll hemorrhage, you should have thought of that before." She sobbed so quietly, but from her gut. You could hear how bad she hurt. Two minutes later, completely traumatized, it was my turn. I passed out even as they anesthetized me, and I woke up about two hours later. All those women, again lined up in a long dirty hallway. Everyone looking around, quiet, some pretty bloody. A while later a nurse came and made us all put on these giant diapers and line up at the pay phone to call someone to pick us up. After my phone call the nurse pulled me aside to tell me they may not have gotten everything, and if I started bleeding unexpectedly I should give the office a call. For the next couple years I kept imagining a giant baby arm growing inside me and then having to give birth to it.

Whether or not my next tale is related no one will ever know, as every last one of my medical records, from three different hospitals, is MIA. I never existed, medically, before 2000. After high school, I started getting very sick. My skin was sapped of all color. Sleeping was the only thing I could do for more than a couple of hours, and to stand upright caused me so much pain it was unbelievable. Once, my period went on for two months. I would go to the emergency room to see a doctor—without insurance there is no other way. And while by law they have to see you, they make you wait all day. After spending five minutes with me, the nurse or doctor would send me home with a package of birth control and a few brochures about sex that made me feel like a big whore who deserved to rot from the inside out before I turned twenty-one. One night, after six months of walking around dead, I was having plain old vanilla boyfriend sex when dark blood started pouring out of my vagina like a river. My legs went numb. My poor boyfriend carried me to the car and into the emergency room. We waited all night. Eventually a nurse made me walk to an exam room where she told me to strip and get on the table, a doctor would be in to see me. It was cold, but she gave me no gown. Nothing but a table and a clock in the room. I lay there for almost three hours. A doctor came in and told me I was obese. Then I tried to explain what had been going on with me, and recounted the night's events. She never examined me at all. "Get dressed, you're having sex too rough," she said. "If it hurts, don't do it." She walked out.

In the months to come I just got worse. I was miserable. I was convinced I had some horrible disease and was going to die any day. I made one last attempt at the emergency room, and by chance I got a doctor who actually gave a shit. She wanted an ultrasound, which cost three hundred and fifty dollars at the time. I told her I had no way to pay for it. She ran out of the room, came back with a machine, and told me she would take care of it. On the ultrasound she said something was there, but she could not see it. My stomach was too tender to feel around. I was scheduled for a laparoscopy the next week. Outpatient surgery, small incision in the bellybutton, they slide a camera in and look around. The surgery fell on my birthday, and after I signed my life away they drugged me up and sent me in. When I woke up I couldn't really move too well, but managed to lower the blanket to find not an incision in my bellybutton but a row of metal staples where before I had pubic hair. Twenty staples, on my twentieth birthday. Being all knocked out and delirious, I was convinced they'd done the wrong surgery. A nurse came in with my doctor and they explained in tandem how they'd found a thirteen-pound cyst attached to both my ovaries, and that my fallopian tubes were wrapped around it. They had to take it out before any more damage was done. It was too big to remove through my bellybutton; therefore, my staples. Another nurse came in and showed me my new morphine drip. She slid it into my IV and I spent the next day or so timing out my next hit.

Later they explained what they had done. They took an ovary out, and now I have about one day every two months in which I can conceive. I was told they had to piece my fallopian tubes back together, so there was a chance that, if I ever did get pregnant, it would be tubal, in which case I could try and have the baby relocated to my uterus. They also had failed to mention earlier that they severed all the muscles in my lower abdomen, so afterward my stomach just hung down, like I had been through a few babies. In fact I walked around kind of holding on to it, like it was my baby instead of my saggy, deserted womb.

After that, I explain, it has been worse and better, but I have never really felt good. My audience of medical professionals and trainees is gazing at me as though they would like to slit my wrists for me, just to make it stop. I ask if they need me to say more, and they all look at each other, shake their heads, and the nurse proclaims me worthy of my prescription. When they ask me my dosage I double it, and head to the pharmacy upstairs. Only a five-hour wait if I need 'em tonight . . .

THE POET AND THE PAUPER

Meliza Bañales

Growing up, there were hundreds of times when I wanted to be a writer. I must have decided on it in seventh grade, when my grandparents got me an electric typewriter for my birthday. I had been writing poems on Grandma Petersen's card table and I suppose she felt there was a more productive way of doing things. That typewriter followed me until my freshman year of college, and even then it was hard to give it up to the dawning of the computer age. But I went with the times.

I have been a writer, professional and otherwise, for much of my life, and my only hope was that someday I would be good at it. I thought publishing was nice, but I knew I would be a writer whether I published or not.

In the Laundromat recently, I met a famous poet. He lives in Berkeley and writes poems about trees. He is very published, about eighty or so publications to his credit, including four books of poems. He has been interviewed for *Poets and Writers*, has taught poetry through NEA grants, and has read with some great people, like John Ashbery. I'm sure he must have felt he knew something about me when he began to talk to me at the top of the wash cycle. He recognized my name, asked where I was getting my M.F.A. I told him I had just graduated from San Francisco State. He told me he remembered that I edited a magazine once, that I rejected one of his poems, but that another editor after me published one. I told him I didn't remember. I have edited magazines and scripts for a long time now, five years, and I couldn't place him right away. But I told him that I was sure his work was nice.

He asked me what I wrote. I get asked this question a lot and I never really know what to say: family, magic, poor people, brown people, mixed-race, family. It's never so black and white, I think. But people want to know, and the famous writer asked me in the Laundromat if I was published and what I was doing with my writing. I told him I had a book coming out, a book of poems. It would be out in one week. Again, he asked me what I wrote about. I told him the same subjects, and he looked at me as if he had a sour taste in his mouth. He said, "Huh, all that? There's not really a huge market for poor people. You probably won't do too well, especially since it's your first book. How did *you* get a book deal?"

The words fell, stones in a lake. They sank and the farther down they went, the more I could feel their weight, their overwhelming weight, crushing me. It was not the first time someone had told me this. I've been told by various people, in various ways, that I have nothing to say. I've been on stages all over the country and even outside of the United States and have been told to "fuck off" and asked "what do you think you're doing?" I've collected all of these and placed them as artifacts in my work, remnants of a typical life. But when the famous writer asked me the question during the spin cycle, all I could do was taste potatoes.

My mother was a master of all things potato. We grew up that broke. She would sometimes dig in trash cans for bottles and cans, because she was too proud to go on welfare. Then she would take the recycling money to the Lucky's grocery store down the street and buy a bag of potatoes. We would eat them mashed, creamed, chunky, in soup, even potato sandwiches. As a kid they stuck to my throat, never coming out.

The famous writer was still waiting for an answer. I was stuck in a bucket of memory. My brothers and I hiding our yellow tickets at school, never telling anyone we got "free lunch." Trips to Kmart to buy four children school clothes. Living in a one-bedroom apartment, one large bed supporting three tired bodies. My days spent wishing I was a real princess in a palace, eating French fries and watching cable TV in my own room. I looked for a moment, something to give the poet. But none of them seemed to make it real. I wanted to break down the racism, the classism, the outright rude nature of the poet's question, his comments like seared grease on a frying pan that just wouldn't come clean.

I wanted to let him know that I knew how to say "fuck you" without ever uttering the words. I wanted him to know what your own self-pity can taste like, how having nothing made you only want more, so much more that you were willing to imagine yourself somewhere else every day of your life. How you dreamed of being in a different-colored skin or a different culture, how you wished your father could speak more clearly, how you hated your mother for never sticking up for herself and staying in jobs that spat on her self-worth. How you saw living as a luxury and surviving as a reality. How you chewed at your own fingers until they bled and held the wounds in your mouth to remind yourself that you had control over something. The famous poet wanted me to tell him how it happened, how I came to this, to be in books and in universities; to be the judge of literature when I came from nothing, which really meant I had nothing, which equaled I was nothing.

Of course, I said nothing. I didn't tell him about the memories. Instead, I smiled. I smiled because as a woman, as a woman of color, as a poor woman of color, I didn't want to be impolite. I smiled because I wanted the poet to know that I was schooled in the art of getting by, that I had spent years learning and perfecting this smile I was giving him. The same smile my Mexican father gave to white people every time he was passed over for promotions or raises, or on the street. The same smile my mother gave her male bosses at work when they made "secretary" out to mean "personal slave," when their glances and passes at her came daily and she smiled because she had a family and no education and losing her job was just not an option. The smile my sister gave her own husband when he called her "stupid" and "fat" only hours after she gave birth to their second child. The smile my brother, Eddie, gives the cops even though he's been out of prison for years, has a good job, and is married. The smile my brother, David, gave his first-grade teacher when she told him that she would be holding him back a year because he read too slowly (she thought he wouldn't understand her speaking English to him anyway, and she didn't hesitate to tell him this to his six-year-old face). The same smile my grandparents, my cousins, my neighborhood always gave to rich white people, people of authority, whenever they were up against the wall with no chance of escape. I wanted to take all of those smiles and throw them at the poet, to let him know that I came from a different sort of education, one where you never let them know how much they get to you, never let them know how deep they've cut your soul.

But I just smiled, retrieved my wet clothes from the machine, and began placing them into another. I felt like I had failed. I hated smiling. Through all of my feminist awareness, my life experience, my existence, all I could come up with was a smile. I felt defeated and ashamed. And there were my mother's potatoes, clawing at the back of my throat, wanting desperately to come out. To throw up a potato potpie filled with the starch taste of want.

My clothes dried. I folded. I kept my mouth shut. The famous poet finished his laundry and left, waving to me as if I were an old friend. I went back to my car, where I decided that he was right: There is no market for poor people. And I returned to his question: How did *you* get a book deal?

In essence, it didn't make sense. I come from poor, working-class roots. My parents weren't college-educated. I grew up in the ghetto, the slums, the part of town people know exists but never see. I didn't write about trees, or language, or literature. For a long time, I didn't know about rhyme and meter or sound in a poem. I hadn't been brought up on the great authors of the canon and I didn't write every day because I was too busy working two jobs or trying to be the first in my family to go to college. I wrote about things I knew. I put my grandmother into my poems—her stories, her voice. I wrote about the days she spent beating her laundry against a rock and losing everything to the Dust Bowl of the 1930s. I wrote about my father's parents, who believed in magic and ghosts and the Pope and who worked in the fields of California and Texas for more than eighty years. I wrote about my sister, her unbreakable strength, how her touch still remained tender through years of abuse. I wrote about my parents, their struggle to make every day special for us, to make it seem like we had everything we needed. How I grew up with few worries when it came to love and affection and a home that I wanted to be in. According to the famous poet in the Laundromat—the poet who had eighty publications, wrote about trees, read with John Ashbery—according to him, poetry had no room for me, for my life. According to him, nobody wanted to read about my family, my poor, brown, mestiza family. Nobody cared about roses in concrete, or love through traffic. Poetry was a place that had no room for these subjects. The fact that, amid the patriarchy, racism, classism, homophobia, and ageism of this society, I was able to get a book published that did not represent these structures, but worked against them, made me see that maybe the famous poet's question was appropriate. How did I do this. How did I get here. How did this come to be.

My answer came a few days later. That night, after doing my laundry, I went home to my boifriend, my FTM transgender boifriend (something I'm sure the poet would have asked me about as well if he had known), and cried in his arms. I told him how the poet called me out and all I did was smile. My boifriend told me it was the smartest thing I could have done. The poet wouldn't have listened to anything I said anyway. It was like that, my boifriend concluded. Smiling was not failing. In a way, I had been passing. I had been undercover. When I was discovered, smiling was all that was left because it didn't have to explain itself. It was just a smile. Take it or leave it.

Sitting down to write this, I come to an answer, and if the famous poet ever reads this he can hold me to every word. How did I get a book deal? How am I able to be in books and universities? How is it that my poems find themselves in print? I believe it's because it's poetry. Poetry is real. It encourages connections and wants attention. In the words of Muriel Rukeyser, from her book *The Life of Poetry*, "A poem invites a total response." My family, my life, is worthy of a total response. Though the oppressions of American culture remain, they are not what completely dominate a readership of poetry. I suppose I could say that my book

getting published is proof that people are interested in this type of work
and that there is a desire for its existence. I've spent much of my time
feeling as though what I was writing was not "real" poetry. In the course
of achieving three degrees, all of them in creative writing and literature, I
have been told in many ways that what I write is "too ethnic," "too confes-
sional," "too limited to only one experience," and "too raw." I was even told
by a professor who I respected and looked up to as a mentor that I should
reconsider going into an M.F.A. program. "Your work may not fit most
programs," he told me, because it just doesn't "read like the poetry being
published today." He feared I would walk away disappointed. I will say that
all of these criticisms have come from white men who have numerous cre-
dentials and are taken seriously by other poets and critics. For a long time,
I internalized these "critiques," this free "advice" they were giving me.
These poets felt they were helping me, doing me a favor. I almost believed
that they were. Reading countless anthologies, magazines, and new books
of poetry, I began to see what they saw: I did not write like the poets being
published today. My professor, like the famous poet in the Laundromat,
was right. But I don't see this as negatively as they do. I don't want to write
anything that doesn't have the power to make me think and to allow me
to be the decent human being I know I can be.

I'm sure writing about trees and language and literature is very
important. I'm sure there are readers out there who crave that work. But
I can't write that way, I won't write that way. Why does that set me up for
failure? How is writing about "real life," especially my life or how I see the
world, a setup for disappointment? I want to make it clear that the longer
I am kept out of the conversation of poetry, the more I don't exist. The
longer my poems are encouraged to be something they're not, the more
I don't exist.

I wish I could chalk up the famous poet's comments, my professor's
comments, all of the comments I have received from readers who have not
taken the time to truly give my work a "total response" to simple old-
fashioned jealousy. I wish I had an ego that worked that way. I don't.
Really. And to excuse these comments as just "poet jealousy" would be
unjust. Writing off the comments as coming from a place of jealousy

forces the real issues of oppression and prejudice to go undiscussed. There is a much deeper well here. If we look farther down, we will see the bottom, the place where more than water rests. I am one out of hundreds of poets who are just as talented as, if not more talented than, me, who happened to get the dumb luck of being offered a book deal at the age of twenty-five. Me: that mixed-race, Chicana, poor, working-class, queer girl who writes about her brother's lowrider and her dying grandfather. I don't know how fate decided on this. I don't know how on earth I was chosen out of all these writers to be the recipient of such luck.

But I do know that I have earned the right to the poems I imagine. I am as hard-working and broken and human as the next person, despite my complex identity. I don't claim to know everything, but I know some things and I know them well enough to explore them and honor them through poetry. I don't focus on "why me." Rather, I take it as it comes, and please know, Mr.-Famous-Poet-from-the-Laundromat, that I am worthy.

STEAL AWAY

Dorothy Allison

My hands shake when I am hungry, and I have always been hungry. Not for food—I have always had enough biscuit fat to last me. In college I got breakfast, lunch, and dinner with my dormitory fees, but my restless hunger didn't abate. It was having only four dollars till the end of the month and not enough coming in then. I sat at a lunch table with the girls who planned to go to the movies for the afternoon, and counting three dollars in worn bills the rest in coins over and over in my pocket. I couldn't go see any movies.

I went, instead, downtown to steal. I became what had always been expected of me—a thief. Dangerous, but careful. Wanting everything, I tamed my anger, smiling wide and innocently. With the help of that smile I stole toilet paper from the Burger King rest room, magazines from the lower shelves at 7-Eleven, and sardines from the deli—sliding those little cans down my jeans to where I had drawn the cuffs tight with rubber bands. I lined my pockets with plastic bags for a trip to the local Winn Dixie, where I could collect smoked oysters from the gourmet section and fresh grapes from the open bins of produce. From the hobby shop in the same shopping center I pocketed metal snaps to replace the rubber bands on my pantleg cuffs and metal guitar picks I could use to pry loose and switch price tags on items too big to carry away. Anything small enough to fit a palm walked out with me, anything round enough to fit an armpit, anything thin enough to carry between my belly and belt. The smallest, sharpest, most expensive items rested behind my teeth, behind that smile that remained my ultimate shield.

On the day that I was turned away from registration because my scholarship check was late, I dressed myself in my Sunday best and went downtown to the Hilton Hotel. There was a Methodist Outreach Convention with meetings in all the ballrooms, and a hospitality suite. I walked from room to room filling a JCPenney shopping bag with cut-glass ashtrays showing the Hilton logo and faceted wineglasses marked only with the dregs of grape juice. I dragged the bag out to St. Pete beach and sailed those ashtrays off the pier like frisbees. Then I waited for sunset to toss the wineglasses high enough to see the red and purple reflections as they flipped end over end. Each piece shattered ecstatically on the tar-black rocks under the pier, throwing up glass fragments into the spray. Sight and sound, it was better than a movie.

The president of the college invited all of the scholarship students over for tea or wine. He served cheese that had to be cut from a great block with delicate little knives. I sipped wine, toothed cheese, talked politely, and used my smile. The president's wife nodded at me and put her pink fleshy hand on my shoulder. I put my own hand on hers and gave one short squeeze. She started but didn't back away, and I found myself giggling at her attempts to tell us all a funny story. She flushed and told us how happy she was to have us in her home. I smiled and told her how happy I was to have come, my jacket draped loosely over the wineglasses I had hooked in my belt. Walking back to the dorm, I slipped one hand into my pocket, carefully fingering two delicate little knives.

Junior year my scholarship was cut yet again, and I became nervous that working in the mailroom wouldn't pay for all I needed. St. Vincent de Paul offered me a ransom, paying a dime apiece for plates and trays carted off from the cafeteria. Glasses were only good for three cents and hard to carry down on the bus without breaking, but sheets from the alumni guest-room provided the necessary padding. My roommate complained that I made her nervous, always carrying boxes in and out. She moved out shortly after Christmas, and I chewed my nails trying to figure out how to carry her mattress down to St. Vincent de Paul. I finally decided it was hopeless, and spent the rest of the holidays reading Jean Genet and walking through the art department hallways.

They had hardwood stools in the studios, and stacking file boxes no one had opened in years. I wore a cloth cap when I took them, and my no-nonsense expression. I was so calm that one of the professors helped me clear paper off the third one. He was distracted, discussing Jackson Pollock with a very pale woman whose hands were marked with tusche. "Glad they finally decided to get these out of here," was all he said to me, never once looking up into my face. My anger came up from my stomach with an acid taste. I went back for his clipboard and papers, but his desk was locked and my file broke on the rim. In compensation I took the silk lining out of the pockets of the corduroy coat he'd left thrown over a stool. The silk made a lemongrass sachet I gave my mother for her birthday, and every time I saw him in that jacket I smiled.

My sociology professor had red hair, forty shelves of books, four children, and an entirely cordial relationship with her ex-husband. When she invited me to dinner, I did not understand what she wanted with me. I watched her closely and kept my hands in my pockets. She talked about her divorce and the politics in the department, how she had worked for John F. Kennedy in 1960 and demonstrated for civil rights in Little Rock in '65. There were lots of books she could lend me, she insisted, but didn't say exactly which ones. She poured me Harveys Bristol Cream, trailing her fingers across my wrist when I took the glass. Then she shook her head nervously and tried to persuade me to talk about myself, interrupting only to get me to switch topics as she moved restlessly from her rocking chair to her bolster to the couch beside me. She did not want to hear about my summers working in the mop factory, but she loved my lies about hitch-hiking cross-country.

"Meet me for lunch on Monday," she insisted, while her eyes behind her glasses kept glancing at me, turning away and turning back. My palms were sweaty, but I nodded yes. At the door she stopped me, and put her hand out to touch my face.

"Your family is very poor, aren't they?"

My face froze and burned at the same time. "Not really," I told her, "not anymore." She nodded and smiled, and the heat in my face went down my body in waves.

I didn't want to go on Monday but made myself. Her secretary was confused when I asked about lunch. "I don't have anything written down about it," she said, without looking up at her calendar.

After class that afternoon the sociology professor explained her absence with a story about one of her children who had been bitten by a dog, but not seriously. "Come on Thursday," she insisted, but on Thursday neither she nor her secretary were there. I stood in the doorway to her office and tilted my head back to take in her shelves of books. I wanted to pocket them all, but at the same time I didn't want anything of hers. Trembling, I reached and pulled out the fattest book on the closet shelf. It was a hardbound edition of *Sadism at the Movies,* with a third of the pages underlined in red. It fit easily in my backpack, and I stopped in the Student Union bookstore on the way back to the dorm to buy a Hershey bar and steal a bright blue pen.

On the next Monday, she apologized again, and again invited me to go to lunch the next day. I skipped lunch but slipped in that afternoon to return her book, now full of my bright blue comments. In its spot on the shelf there was now a collection of the essays of Georges Bataille, still unmarked. By the time I returned it on Friday, heavy blue ink stains showed on the binding itself.

Eventually we did have lunch. She talked to me about how hard it was to be a woman alone in a college town, about how all the male professors treated her like a fool, and yet how hard she worked. I nodded.

"You read so much," I whispered.

"I keep up," she agreed with me.

"So do I," I smiled.

She looked nervous and changed the subject but let me walk her back to her office. On her desk, there was a new edition of Malinowski's *The Sexual Life of Savages*. I laid my notebook down on top of it, and took them both when I left. Malinowski was a fast read. I had that one back a day later. She was going through her date book looking for a free evening we could have dinner. But exams were coming up so soon. I smiled and nodded and backed out the door. The secretary, used to seeing me come and go, didn't even look up.

I took no other meals with professors, didn't trust myself in their houses. But I studied their words, gestures, jokes, and quarrels to see just how they were different from me. I limited my outrage to their office shelves, working my way through their books one at a time, carefully underlining my favorite passages in dark blue ink—occasionally covering over their own faded marks. I continued to take the sociology professor's classes but refused to stay after to talk, and when she called my name in the halls, I would just smile and keep walking. Once she sat beside me in a seminar and put her hand on the back of my neck where I was leaning back in my chair. I turned and saw she was biting her lips. I remembered her saying, "Your family is very poor, aren't they?" I kept my face expressionless and looked forward again. That was the afternoon I made myself a pair of harem pants out of the gauze curtains from the infirmary.

My parents came for graduation, Mama taking the day off from the diner, my father walking slow in his back brace. They both were bored at the lunch, uncomfortable and impatient to have the ceremony be over so we could pack my boxes in the car and leave. Mama kept pulling at the collar of my robe while waiting for the call for me to join my class. She was so nervous she kept rocking back on her heels and poked my statistics professor with her elbow as he tried to pass.

"Quite something, your daughter," he grinned as he shook my mama's hand. Mama and I could both tell he was uncomfortable, so she just nodded, not knowing what to say. "We're expecting great things of her," he added, and quickly joined the other professors on the platform, their eyes roaming over the parents headed for the elevated rows at the sides and back of the hall. I saw my sociology professor sharing a quick sip from the dean's pocket flask. She caught me watching, and her face flushed a dull reddish gray. I smiled widely as ever I had, and held that smile through the long slow ceremony that followed, the walk up to get my diploma, and the confused milling around that followed the moment when we were all supposed to throw our tassels over to the other side. Some of the students threw their mortarboards drunkenly into the air, but I tucked mine under my arm and found my parents before they had finished shaking the cramps out of their legs.

"Sure went on forever," Mama whispered, as we walked toward the exit.

The statistics professor was standing near the door telling a tall black woman, "Quite something, your son. We're expecting great things of him."

I laughed and tucked my diploma in Mama's bag for the walk back to the dormitory. People were packing station wagons, U-Haul trailers, and bulging little sedans. Our Pontiac was almost full and my face was starting to ache from smiling, but I made a quick trip down into the dormitory basement anyway. There was a vacuum cleaner and two wooden picture frames I'd stashed behind the laundry-room doors that I knew would fit perfectly in the Pontiac's trunk. Mama watched me carry them up but said nothing. Daddy only laughed and revved the engine while we swung past the auditorium. At the entrance to the campus I got them to pull over and look back at the scattered buildings. It was a rare moment, and for a change my hunger wasn't bothering me at all. But while my parents waited, I climbed out and pulled the commemorative roses off the welcome sign. I got back in the car and piled them into my mama's lap.

"Quite something, my daughter," she laughed, and hugged the flowers to her breast. She rocked in her seat as my stepfather gunned the engine and spun the tires pulling out. I grinned while she laughed.

"Quite something."

It was the best moment I'd had in four years.

FARM USE

Joy Castro

After the divorce, my mother's first entrepreneurial effort fails. She opens a resale clothing shop and gives it a clever name: Encore. But in small-town West Virginia, people's used finery is a shabby thing. Her clientele has none of the chic-girl-down-on-her-luck wit the name deserves. Instead of Jean Rhys heroines, she attracts fat, bad-smelling women who slap their kids. There is nothing vintage to find. Her racks hold only the same clothes that once hung at Hill's and Heck's, the budget department stores. But they're dingier, with the smell of stale closets. At the counter, irritated women claim their things are worth more than my mother thinks.

Even in the black-and-white wedding photos, my mother's eyes have a touch of sleaze, a come-hither Joan Collins glint. My father's face is young, eager, shining; he looks toward her. She looks at the camera, chin lowered, one white satin toe pointed forward, eyes leveling their invitation.

Once she and some other stewardesses partied on a yacht with O. J. Simpson, she tells me when I'm nine. I think how much fun it would be: throwing footballs on the deck, eating cake all day.

His hands are furred black, his head bald and shiny, his gut a fat ball under graying T-shirts. He buys my brother Tonka trucks, buys me the radio I crave, buys my mother clothes and me a plum velvet blazer, very grown-up, for wearing to the Kingdom Hall. "Won't it be nice," my mother purrs, "to use the child support your father sends just on school clothes and nice things, instead of bills?"

She's got us there. I'm sick of food stamps and government cheese and clothes discarded by strangers. Middle school is a bad time to be poor. And I'm tall for my age and pretty. At assemblies, eighteen-year-old brothers from other congregations flirt with me between sessions, ask my mother if they can take me out. They back away, apologizing, when they learn I'm twelve. I want a black leather clutch purse and combs for my hair.

But not this way. I argue with her, but things move quickly. He makes fourteen dollars an hour working construction. He's a respected brother; he's served at Bethel. A date is set. I'm to wear my plum velvet blazer. My brother, seven, is to give her away in the ceremony at our Kingdom Hall.

"Won't that be cute?" she says.

"No, not really," I say.

I cry in her room as she dresses, begging her not to do it, not to do it, but I have no evidence aside from the weird way he looks at us. She's patient for a while, going over the money he makes, the good reputation he has in his congregation—but finally she turns on me.

"I am just about fed up, you hear? Do you understand me? I've just about had it with your bellyaching." She swings the hairbrush in my face. "Why do you always want to ruin everything? Why? One good thing comes along, something that will actually make me happy for once, and you have to start your whining. As usual."

"He's not a good man." I'm still crying. She laughs angrily, throws the brush down on the bureau.

"What do you know about good men? You're twelve years old." Her voice is rich with disgust. "Do you think you know what a good man is? Do you?" She shakes me. "Well?" I just cry. "Do you think your *father's* a good man?" I look at the brown and green carpet.

"Yes."

She stares at me, then lets me loose with a final shake and turns her back. She steps into the silky fawn dress.

"Well, that just shows what you know." It's early in the day, but the wide straps of her bra are already gouging into her shoulders, scoring the red welts we see when she changes into her nightgown at night. She tosses her head, talks to the mirror. "You listen here. I'm getting married today, and there's nothing, absolutely nothing, that you can do about it. Do you hear me?"

"Yes."

"For your information, young lady, I am happy. You can be happy, too, or you can sit in the corner and snivel. Is that clear?"

"Yes."

When the elder asks, "Who gives this woman in marriage?" my brother, confused, must be prodded to speak. "I do," he says, worried, his eyes casting about to see if he's done the right thing.

The promised wealth does not materialize. Our stepfather visits numerous doctors until one agrees to sign the papers that say he has black lung. He has bullied our mother into selling her share of the store, into selling our house, into buying a trailer and moving hours away to a trailer park in a small town where we know no one.

The first disability check arrives. He stops working, stays home. He's constantly there, watching.

The money problems worsen. Our clothes are not replaced. We start the new school shabby, in castoffs. If we want clothes for school, he tells us, we can have a yard sale, sell our toys. Our mother urges us to comply; we'll feel so much better if we have some nice things.

All Saturday we sit in the yard. Strange kids pick up my horse models, my brother's Matchbox cars and Tonka trucks. One by one the items go, my plastic family of smoke-gray Arabians scattered.

We make almost a hundred dollars. It can buy new shoes for both of us, new pants for my brother, maybe a sweater for me.

My stepfather takes the stacks of ones. There will be no clothes. Everything that's ours, he says, is his. Get used to it.

We go to school ragged, mismatched, hopeless.

✳   ✳   ✳

In rural areas, the occasional truck has Farm Use painted on its sides, a special dispensation to relieve the family farm of the expenses of a license, insurance.

In the back, sometimes, gaunt children ride, their arms wrapped tiredly around their knees, hunched amid bales or firewood or piles of scrap. They stare dead-eyed into the car behind.

My brother and I are those children. Our arms are wrapped around our knees. Our stepfather drives our Farm Use truck all over town: to the post office, the grocery. We sit in the back, staring at children belted safely into seats beside their parents. Sometimes, they're children from school, children we know. They point, talk to their parents excitedly, stare at us in fascination and disgust.

My ass is a moving target. I cannot pass the couch without a slap, a pinch, a long stroke that ends in squeezing. I walk as quickly, straightly, as invisibly as I can. "This girl of yours sure does love to wiggle, don't she, Mother?" he calls to the kitchen.

"Yes, she does," comes a deadened voice.

As time passes, the rules intensify. Work is a punishment; after school, we clear brush until we cannot see to sickle. We carry wood. Dig ditches for the gas lines. Food becomes a measured thing. Each mealtime, my stepfather dishes himself up from the pots. Then my mother may help herself to half of what he has taken. Then, while he watches, she can spoon half of what she's taken onto my plate. A portion half the size of mine goes to my brother. If my stepfather wants one peanut butter and jelly sandwich, my brother gets one-eighth. If she gives us more than my stepfather calculates is correct, he beats us with his belt.

We sit at dinner, our eyes on our plates. If we look our stepfather in the eye, ever, without being told to, we're beaten.

"How those little titties of yours doing?" he says to me. "They must be sprouting pretty good right about now."

If I do not keep eating, I'll have stomach pains later, or I'll have to eat dry the packets of Carnation Instant Breakfast we all get free in gym and which the other girls leave lying in their lockers.

After class, I try to make my voice casual. "Are you going to eat that?" I say, pointing.

They look at each other, grinning. Then back at me, their eyes cool and repelled. "No. My god. Take it if you want it."

You're supposed to pour it in milk, but I have no milk. On the school bus, I sink down so no one can see me and rip the top back, pour the dry grains in my mouth, chew. I learn to like it.

"Must be like two puppies. Isn't that right, Mother?"

"Yes."

"Two puppies with brown noses."

Something in my throat is clogging, but I chew, eyes down, head down. My brother keeps eating. I feel my mother's gaze like a beam of heat in my hair.

Doing dishes, I palm a steak knife from the kitchen, easing the drawer silently open, sliding it into my pocket. In bed, I slide it under the side pillow, practice grabbing it in the dark, my hand darting to catch its handle fast as a rabbit's dash.

He finds it, lying beside me in the darkness as he has begun to do, breathing, his whole body stiff and heavy in the bed next to me. First, on top of the bedspread. Now under the sheets.

I think of nothing. I do not pray. I lie there in a stillness so extreme I might be dead, each nerve a wire humming with still terror.

"What's this?" he says. He sits up. "Turn that light on." I do. The room jumps to brightness, and I pull my arm back to my side. Only my eyes swerve to see the knife gripped in his hand.

"What you got this for, girly?"

I look at the window, the door, long for my mother to appear. "It's so isolated here. I get afraid. Of robbers, I mean." My voice is strangled, unbelievable.

"Is that so?" His grin leaks slowly across his mouth. It's a good game, cat and mouse. "Robbers."

"Yes. It's isolated here," I say.

"Well, no robbers are gonna get you. I'm here. I'm here to protect my little girl. You don't need this." He rises and moves around the bed to stand above me. "We don't want you cutting yourself by accident, do we? A sharp knife like this?" He holds the blade in my face. I push my head back into the pillow.

"No, sir," I whisper.

"Then I'll just take this back to the kitchen." Quick as a fox, his free hand reaches out and flips back the blankets, unzips my quilted pink nightgown, sternum to crotch, flips the fabric open. He stares down at me, my breasts, my hipbones, my white underwear. His eyes glitter. He grins down for a minute.

"So cover yourself up," he says. My hands fly to my waist, but the zipper snags, sticks, jerks upward. "Don't be so modest," he laughs. "Fathers have a right to see their daughters. It's natural." The corners of the room are thick with shadow. "And what am I?"

"My spiritual father," I whisper. I am a wax doll, empty, pliant, a cunning image of the girl who used to live here.

"That's right." The lamp clicks. The darkness becomes deeper darkness. "No more knives. You hear?"

"Yes, sir."

His steps shake the trailer as he moves down the hall.

The way to make my stepfather a pie is this. First, you make the crust, the light, flaking, curling crust he requires every day. My mother does this with her family recipe and sets it aside. I meet her at the table in the yard, each of us holding a small knife.

Then you peel the apples—the small, sweet ones, the kind he likes, I don't know their names, I'm not allowed in the grocery store—and then you cut them in half, top to bottom, straight through the center. Then you cut the halves in half. Then you scoop the core out with the knife, following the lines in the apple's pale meat. Then you slice the cored quarters.

The slices will go into the crust, the dish will go into the oven, two pieces, hot, will go into their bowls, and his will get a scoop of Breyer's vanilla ice cream. Many times he tells us it's the best ice cream, as BMW is the best motorbike and Nikon is the best camera. Both of which he has. "Bavarian Motor Works," he likes to bellow, apropos of nothing.

My brother and I do not eat pie. It is a punishment. "Five desserts!" our stepfather yells when we err, leaping triumphantly to his feet to make the little marks, /////, on the sheet pinned to the wall for that purpose. When I run away, I am up to minus seventy-six desserts. We never get to zero. When we get close, he's more watchful. He loves to let us get to two or three.

It's fall. He's inside watching television. My mother and I sit in the yard, peeling, coring, slicing. The glossy apples disappear under our knives, emerge as neat pale slivers lying flat in the dish. I feel the slight resistance of the flesh, then the final quick *thunk* as blade hits board.

"I don't know what I'm going to do," she says in a low smothered voice.

I carve a red curling spiral away from the flesh. She glances at me, sighs noisily. "I just don't know what I'm going to do."

"What about?"

"About him."

I think she's going to talk about running again. I'm sick of running, sick of waking up in the motel bed to hear her whispering into the phone, promising, apologizing, giving him directions. I'm sick of the pains in my stomach when we head back east again. Maybe she's starting to plan, I think. But we have no car to run in now. He sold it after the last time. We're ten miles outside a little town in rural West Virginia. We know no one but Witnesses.

And we've been through that, spent nights at elders' houses, the blood drying on her lip, her eye blacked, my brother bruised and shaking, the two of us huddled silent on a strange couch. They send us home. It's a family situation, a private matter. They acknowledge the rule my stepfather holds over her like a swinging blade: Except in cases of adultery, a wife cannot divorce her husband. It's a sin. We go back.

But leaving isn't on her mind.

"I don't know what it's going to take." My quarters fall into clean fans of slices, which I gather and drop in the dish.

"What what's going to take?"

"What it's going to take to satisfy him."

My knife steadies itself against the board. "Meaning what?"

"He's never satisfied." Her voice drops to a whisper. "Nothing I do." She pushes a long lock of gray back from her face. All the curl's fallen out of it since he's made her grow it out. "Three, four times a day he wants it."

I cut my last apple through its center.

"You're a big girl. You know what I mean."

The halves into halves. The half-moons of the cores, the pith and seeds into the pot of waste.

"I could lose my mind," she says, her voice breaking. I stop cutting and look up. She's crying, but her hands don't stop moving. I can hear the creek. My brother is scything weeds in the distance. "I think it might kill me or something." She keeps her eyes on her apple, her knife. The trees rise dark up the mountain behind her. "He needs some other kind of— some kind of outlet." The only sound is her knife hitting the board as the slices separate.

I stare at her, at the wide dark bowl of the valley we live in. She glances up at me, then at the dish of apples.

"Here, have one," she says, fishing out a slice. Even though apples have been forbidden to my brother and me for months, I can remember their taste, their sour springing juice. She shakes it at me anxiously, glances at the trailer windows. For him to see this would mean a beating—for me, at least, if not for her.

"I think I'm done," I say, and stand up.

RAIN

Ida Acton

Oh god that summer. So fuckin' hot you never wanted to even move. You just lay in the shade and breathed shallow. Like not even trying to let that hot fuckin' air into your lungs anyway. The lawn was dead and brown where it used to be green, and growing over everything since the mower broke. The paint-peeling house just squatted in the center of all that dead grass like an unhappy doomed thing. It was the summer we all prayed for rain. Prayed for it in church, prayed for it every morning at breakfast after Momma read the daily Bible chapter and you wiped margarine from your fingers with those same napkins y'all had been cartin' around America since you were a baby. Brown with tiny yellow flowers. Smart to make napkins brown, you thought, 'cause of how then they don't show stains, and you were trippin' over the crabby old dog on your way out the door. Counselor at the Vacation Bible School at Momma's church. Which is where all the neighborhood kids went when their folks wanted to keep them from standing in the middle of the street all day. And they were dirty and mucous-y and tattered and grabby and sweet and sticky. Always holding and tugging. And wanting and needing. And you were knucklin' the sleep out the corners of yer eyes and just trying to keep all those little terrors in line as you rolled your eyes heavenward and daydreamed of rain. Every step you took sent rivers of sweat pouring down under your T-shirt and your feet were like the dry cracked earth themselves, bug-bit and sun-burnt and crammed into those worn-down flat-tire flip-flops. But this is how things always were, midwestern summers and never no AC, just those big-ass fans workin' overtime all day long. After you put in your four unpaid hours of service for the Lord you got to leave the church where you had hid in the relative cool of the basement and got the kids to do cut-and-paste Christian projects. Noah and Moses and a million other waving clean pink-faced cut-out characters in robes. And then you passed out all those white-bread sandwiches. Generic peanut butter and purple jelly. Donated from the food bank. And twenty little mouths are chewing in unison. One for you too, Ida.

Trudging home through all those tiny worn-out dry alleys and the sky was getting gray, you noticed, but the heat still hung on you like tacky too-tight synthetic clothes, bunched and hanging, and you looked up to feel wet drops pissing down and then it just cracked open the whole fuckin' world, the fuckin' sky, it just came apart and it was rivers falling down on you, there. Standing feet apart and mouth open to the heavens, toes curling into your flip-flops and everything brand-new and soaked and you couldn't see a fuckin' thing through those wet glasses no more and you were just there, sodden and blind and it just kept coming like that, turning the dust stuck to your skin into rivers of mud down your legs and endless, forever, just rain. And you were free in that fuckin' alley, do you remember that, Ida? Free of Vacation Bible School and Jesus and that high school where all those kids hated you. How you looked at nothing but your feet for years. But right then you were free and only you, sixteen and washed away in the alley with all that rain cleaning you out. There was nothing anymore, no obligations, no lingering hopelessness, no shame about being poor. And you were walkin' home with your glasses in your sodden pocket, squinting for stop signs and tripping over your flip-flops, going home to fall dripping into those cotton sheets where you couldn't see the pattern in the middle anymore 'cause you'd been sleeping in the same spot for so many years and laundry always on Saturday had worn all those flower prints away right there, and they were so thin you could see right through them when they hung out on the line. And that's how it always was there: same napkins, same sheets, no money, dead grass and electric fans and a Bible chapter every morning and your great-grand-mother's rocker and margarine in giant 99-cent tubs. And hope grew like weeds after rain there, and grief accumulated like leaves in the gutters, making the rain flood over and stain through the walls.

THE PRISON WE CALLED HOME

Siobhan Brooks

I was born in the Sunnydale housing projects in San Francisco on July 14, 1972. My mother had been living in the Haight Ashbury district, where she used to take pictures of the Bay Bridge from her apartment, but the rents increased and white people moved in, so she had to move. Being a single Black woman without a high school diploma, the projects were the only place she could find to live. And Sunnydale, known for its violence, always had vacancies.

These projects are the largest in San Francisco. Built during World War II, they look like red-and-white row houses. Though they are now predominantly Black (along with a few Asian, Latino, and Samoan families), they weren't always. White people used to live in them during the 1940s, when they functioned as military housing. Then the suburbs were built up, and white people went to live in those communities, keeping Blacks out, locked in the ghetto. It was strange for me to see old photos of Sunnydale with suburban-looking white families living there. The only white people who lived in Sunnydale when I was growing up were white women who mothered Black children and had been rejected from the white world.

Like most projects, Sunnydale had a reputation for violence, and was referred to as "Swampy Desert" or "Swampy D." My mother tried her best to make our unit seem like home. She bought beads, curtains, a birdbath, and marble tables that she ordered from catalogues in order to make the house look nice, in spite of the roaches that lived in the corner of our stove. We covered our food with foil to keep them away. I used to love watching her decorate our place with contact paper, woodprints, plants, and bright fabric that she would sew onto our chairs. She bought the initials **A** and **S** (for Aldean and Siobhan) to place outside our door.

I felt most loved by my mother at Christmas, when she would buy me dozens of gifts—toys, dolls, games, and clothes: Christmas was her way of proving that we weren't poor, even though we lived in the projects. One Christmas she bought a gingerbread house and wrapped it up to surprise me. I was delighted. I had never had a gingerbread house. While we were looking at the frosting and the smiling gingerbread man, I noticed something brown on top of the house, moving. I pointed it out to my mother—it was a roach. My mother threw the gingerbread house across the room, then grabbed a hammer and crushed it to pieces. She said every racial slur toward Black people imaginable—because of her internalized racism, she often blamed her problems on being Black, not on the effects of white racism against us.

Once we were returning home from the circus and there was a horrible car accident. A little girl, also returning from the circus with her parents, got hit by a car and was killed. The driver was drunk, and the car had actually run through a liquor store; the girl was decapitated. As we approached the crowd, my mother, seeing something, led us in a different direction. We heard about the accident later on the news, and a Malcolm X mural was painted where the accident occurred, but there was no discussion as to why there were so many liquor stores in our area.

Another time there was a Black man running from unit to unit in Sunnydale breaking windows. He had been stabbed and wanted someone to call for help. My mother and I were relieved that he didn't break ours. We had bars on our windows to keep people from breaking in, but they also kept us locked in—if there had been a fire, they would have prevented our escape. Even so, we had our place broken into twice, both times through the door.

✳   ✳   ✳

While these events didn't happen every day in the projects, they are reflective of what it is like to grow up in them. Whether you're talking about projects in Los Angeles, San Francisco, Oakland, New Jersey, Philadelphia, New York, or Chicago, they all share the same incarcerating elements. While projects do have elements of culture, community, and resistance, they also have fear, sadness, hopelessness, and dramatically violent events that, no matter how infrequent, stay imprinted in the mind. There is limited access to space, a dearth of businesses, and intense social isolation. I remember riding the bus with my mother and passing banks, schools, and real-estate agencies, not realizing what they were. Most people in the projects carried cash and/or cashed their checks at a check-cashing place. Few people I knew had bank accounts.

The real-estate agencies were partly responsible for why Black people and other people of color could not live in safe housing. They often catered to the white elite, and steered people of color to the houses with the lowest property values. Poor people of color are forced to live in projects. For us, to be working class would have been a step up. We were the prelude to the working class, locked in a ghetto.

Growing up, we didn't have a playground. We went roof-hopping, played hide-and-go-seek in vacant apartment buildings, climbed trees. We tore the boards from the doorways of vacant units and rode them down nearby steps. We ate dirt, pulled sour grass and chewed on it. Later we were told it was called "sour grass" because the dogs peed on it.

Getting Exposure

The first time I entered a real house, I was eleven years old. I had a Filipina friend named Mary who lived a few blocks away, in one of the houses alongside Sunnydale populated mostly by Asians. Mary went to my elementary school; we were in the same third-grade class. I didn't know her well, but I noticed that she would walk the same way as me when my mother picked me up from school and disappear into one of those houses. One day she invited me over, out of the blue, and without asking my mother if it was O.K., I went.

I remember being amazed at how much space Mary and her family had, compared to the one-bedroom unit with the six-foot ceiling my mother and I shared; Mary's house was like a mansion compared to any unit in Sunnydale. They had a garage, four bedrooms (each of her siblings had their own room), a spacious bathroom, a kitchen with tile floors (clean, no roaches), and a living room with a fireplace. I had never seen a house like that except on television. I remember feeling very small in her house. Her mother was sweet, but wary of me in the beginning, watching my every move. Like many immigrants, she had been taught to fear Black people, and I was the first Black person they had ever had in their house. Even though they lived only a few blocks away from us, we lived in different worlds.

Growing up in the projects, it was common for us to refer to where we lived as our "house." My friends would always ask if they could come over to my house, and vice versa; we never said, "Can I come over to your unit?" But after visiting Mary in a real house, I felt how marginal we were in the projects. Things they took for granted, like space, were new to me. Mary's windows opened up to the view of a garden in the back, birds, and blue sky, without bars.

That day Mary's mother made us Rice Krispies Treats, and we played in her garage. It changed my life forever. After being in their house I never wanted to go back to Sunnydale. I continued to visit after school for an hour and play, becoming exposed to a whole new world. Living in the projects is very similar to living on a Native American reservation—the projects are located on poorly kept land, isolated from the rest of society, and controlled by the government. I recently read that HUD builds the houses on reservations as well as in the projects.

For people living in projects, all roads lead to the ghetto. Our whole social world usually does not expand far from it. The schools we attend are often near our neighborhoods, and, because of our lack of property-value-generated revenue, they have poor funding and overcrowded classrooms. Everyone I knew from school lived in a ghetto or not far from one. I hardly ever met middle-class people—Black, Latino/a, Asian, or white. At school we learned more about our social status by the lack of care the teachers gave us. I remember a class where the social sciences teacher just up and left class because he was tired of dealing with us. He was Black, and so were most of the students. During lunch we were not allowed to leave the campus, and we even had security guards standing outside the entrance. Sometimes the principal would use a lock and chain to keep us in. This was during a peak of gang activity in California, and the principal thought it was safer for us to stay inside during lunch. Once I cut class to visit a friend of mine at another school, which was mostly white; I was surprised by the amount of freedom they had. During lunch the students could sit outside on the grass, or leave the campus entirely.

Everywhere we went there was a police presence: school dances, the bus stop, a police helicopter flying over us at night. And we were always crowded into small spaces: the projects, the welfare lines, the bus. We never experienced the larger, open places in San Francisco. With inferior school systems and housing, the projects were often a prelude to the final form of incarceration: jail and prison. A few of the guys I grew up with ended up in jail, on probation, or dead, while the girls ended up single parents on welfare.

Planning My Escape

The older I got, the more I hated Sunnydale and all communities of color like it. This is contradictory to the notion of being "down" with the ghetto, which some confused Black middle- and working-class people glorify and romanticize (often in gangsta rap and narrow Black nationalist ideology)—usually out of some strange guilt at being spared the "Black" experience of growing up in poverty. Living in an anti-Black, self-hating household, it was easy for me to begin to hate where I came from and the people we lived among. Contrary to the popular belief that people live in the projects because they are not ambitious, or because they are too lazy to get out, my mother had very bourgeois values and manners, which I shared. I had already decided that I was not going to live in the projects when I got older, or be like the people who lived there: If you want to succeed, all you need to do is act right, I believed. I didn't understand, at age fourteen, that our oppression had nothing to do with good behavior and everything to do with structural racism and classism.

During my high school years, my mother spared me household chores so that I could focus on my schoolwork, reading, and writing. I was allowed to be selfish in a way most of my friends were not, and in this regard I had more in common with my white friends than my friends of color.

Growing up in a nonworking environment, I had no working-class identity, and actually began to look down on people who were "just workers." I was going to be a thinker, a writer. When I was sixteen I got my first summer job working at the Presidio hospital doing clerical work, and was surprised when my paycheck did not fall on the first or fifteenth of the month, the dates welfare checks came.

I was fed up with the projects, and desperately wanted out. I hated living in fear of my neighbors, in fear of the men when coming home late at night, fearing the sound of helicopters. I hated being so far removed from the central areas of San Francisco. It took me an hour on the bus to get downtown. Cabs would refuse to bring me all the way home, letting me off where the homes ended and Sunnydale began. I decided that I would explore San Francisco on my own and slowly move out of the projects.

Once, when I was sixteen, I rode the buses until I was lost. I knew that I had to learn the city better if I were going to move outside of my racially segregated environment. I got off at a random stop and went into a cafe to get something to drink.

When I opened the door I was surprised and a bit frightened by what I saw: mostly white people eating and drinking coffee. Prior to opening the door I had never been in a predominantly white environment; I had actually only seen white people on television. I remember feeling awkward, looking at the white boy with piercings behind the counter and at the menu of drinks I couldn't pronounce. If I could successfully order a drink in this place, I thought, I could function outside of Sunnydale, since anything outside of Sunnydale was most likely to be white. I slowly walked up to the counter and mumbled that I wanted a cafe au lait, hoping I pronounced it right. He turned about and made my drink. I decided to drink inside the cafe and observe my surroundings. Most of my neighbors would have felt inferior or scared, and so they stayed where they were most comfortable and accepted—the ghetto.

I was reminded of how Blacks in my area feared white people, even though they would never admit it. I went to a Nirvana concert in the early nineties, at a venue near Sunnydale, the Cow Palace. I remember thinking that it was one of the rare times something was actually near us—usually we had to go far from our neighborhood to see a show or access services. Old Black men normally hung in front of neighborhood liquor stores until the wee hours of the morning, but on the evening of the Nirvana concert, mobs of white kids from the suburbs dominated their turf. Instead of the Black men being at their usual spots, these teenage white boys had taken it. It was the first time I actually wanted to see those Black men in front of the liquor store, claiming their space in the face of whiteness.

Escape from the Swamp

I moved out of the projects during my junior year at San Francisco State University, at the age of twenty-two. My longtime friend Jennifer, a white girl from a working-class background, became my housing hook-up. This is usually how people of color avoid racism and find housing. She used to live with a friend of ours near Golden Gate Park, and when she moved out she gave me her room. The rent was only two hundred dollars, but I remember thinking it was a lot of money to save each month. My mother only paid $160 for our unit in the projects, and she was getting government aid. I was scared to move, but took the challenge.

The day I moved out my mother was hurt; though she wanted me to succeed, she didn't want me to leave her. Once she'd even asked me if I was going to get a unit next door. I remember rolling my eyes and sighing, I'd rather die than live here another day. No one really moved out of Sunnydale, which is why my leaving was such a big deal. Most people move within Sunnydale, or to another housing project. I was doing something most people in Sunnydale could only dream of doing: moving into a nice, safe neighborhood outside of the projects.

Later I moved into another area, also through Jennifer, and lived with a white woman named Mary. While the (mainly white) people that I met in this new-world college neighborhood were nice to me, it was obvious to me that they didn't know many people of color, and the ones they did know were the very best of the best, the cream of the crop—not the average person of color. I call this the Super Nigger Syndrome—in order for a Black person to have decent housing, health care, etc., he or she must perform way above normal standards (standards not set for white people). Blacks, non-Black people of color, and whites have all asked me if I am mixed, or even from this country, because I don't act "ghetto."

Reflections on Sunnydale

Four years ago, after my mother died, I returned to Sunnydale, visiting from New York City where I now attend grad school. I am amazed at how trapped I still feel anytime I spend time there. The projects are more than a physical location, they're also a state of mind, and the experience stays with you long after you leave them. Even now, whenever I hear a loud noise, I startle, thinking it's a gunshot. I went back with my friend Jennifer and visited the family that now lives where my mother and I used to live: a grandmother, mother, and daughter. The mother actually remembered my mother and me from when I was little. I was surprised at how different their place looks from when we used to live there. She told me I could visit anytime. After chatting with them, I left, knowing I would not be back.

On my visit I recognized a woman I had gone to middle school with, repeating the pattern of many women there—welfare, living in the projects. I spoke with her, but we didn't have much to say. I learned that a childhood friend of mine had been murdered in a shootout. During that visit I felt that Sunnydale could be anywhere in the United States, in any Third World country; it will never be seen on any postcard from San Francisco, and remains unseen by the elite within the city. I left Sunnydale that day feeling grateful that I was able to escape from the prison I called home for twenty-three years.

A CATHOLIC LEG

Terry Ryan

Many children get the shock of their lives when they discover the truth about Santa Claus and the Easter Bunny. My greatest shock, which had nothing to do with fiction, came when I realized that our family was poor.

The news should have come as no surprise, considering that my parents, Evelyn and Leo (Kelly) Ryan, had ten children to support on Dad's meager pay as a machinist in the small midwestern town of Defiance, Ohio. Still, the precise scene that triggered this awakening is lost to me; in retrospect, many would serve as appropriate epiphanies.

Was it the day in early August 1948 that Mom's labor pains began, and she and Dad raced in our old jalopy not to the hospital, but to the bank to borrow twenty-five dollars?

Twenty-five dollars would pay at least part of the hospital expenses when my mother finally gave birth to her seventh child, Michael, later that day. My parents knew from experience that the total bill would be sixty-five dollars—it had been sixty-five dollars in 1944 when Bruce was born, and in 1946 when I was born; it would be sixty-five dollars in 1950 when Barb was born, and in 1952 when Betsy was born. In 1937, 1939, 1940, and 1942, when Lea Anne, Dick, Bub, and Rog, respectively, came into the world, the bill never topped twenty-three dollars and fifty cents. Only in

1954, when the last of the ten Ryan babies, Dave, was born, would the price shoot up to a phenomenal ninety-five dollars.

Was it the moment in the early fifties when I noticed I happened to be wearing everyone else's clothes, and always had been?

My wardrobe consisted of shoes my older sister Lea Anne had outgrown, shirts and pants formerly worn by my four older brothers, jackets and winter coats donated from relatives as distant as an aunt's sister-in-law's adopted daughter.

Or could it have been any Thursday afternoon in the mid-fifties when I witnessed my lilac-perfumed and white-gloved Aunt Lucy pull up to the curb in her forest green DeSoto to take my mother grocery shopping at the A&P?

It took all those years of Thursdays for me to understand that Aunt Lucy didn't just drive my mother downtown to the market. She in fact paid for two shopping carts of food every week, without fail. My mother was shy in the face of such generosity and chose from the shelves only the most vital and inexpensive items: flour, soap, sugar, bread. It was Aunt Lucy who went hog-wild, filling the carts with hamburger, chicken, eggs, tomatoes, fruit, cereal, cookies, ice cream, sausage, and soup. By the age of ten, I realized that without the weekly visits of our beloved aunt, we would surely have gone hungry.

Then again, how about the night when I was closing in on seven years old and stood in the doorway of the kitchen watching my burly red-headed father drink himself into a raging stupor, as he did every evening, on whiskey and beer?

It occurred to me then that he was consuming something far more dear than alcohol. At least a third of his weekly paycheck evaporated in this way, and perhaps more. Not to mention the effect of the drinking on his disposition. He roared his way through the night, a shot glass in one hand and a beer bottle in the other, in a mad monologue that could be heard a half a block away. An inebriated Dad was, as my mother used to say, "about as affable as a bee-stung bear," a generous quote that makes him sound almost charming. He certainly could be—when he was sober, when he put his mind to it.

He had an Irish love of words and music, and a talent for entertaining that had surfaced when he was quite young. In his twenties, Dad played the violin and sang with a roving dance band that toured northwestern Ohio. I don't think he ever imagined he'd eventually have to forfeit his free-as-a-bird life of laughter, drink, and dance to toil in a machine shop forty hours a week.

Granted, my father worked hard every day, under pre-OSHA conditions—no ear plugs, no goggles, no heavy aprons, no steel-toed shoes. As a machinist at a locally owned plant called Serrick's, he tended a stationary screw machine ten times his size that consumed buckets of oil and melted solid bars of metal, re-forming them into bits of useful hardware, such as screws, nuts, and bolts. Serrick's had a score of these metallic monsters, lined up in rows, forming a perfectly aligned orchard of steel. Their collective vibratory roar was known to loosen leaves from neighboring trees.

Dad would arrive home every afternoon with hot-oil burns and bits of metal embedded in his clothes, skin, and hair. The grease, which caused boils on his wide, pink, freckled arms, never washed out of his work shirts and pants. His shoes fairly squished when he walked. He once dropped an unwieldy hunk of heavy metal on his feet, crushing his shoes and maiming his toenails for life. But he never missed a day of work because of drinking.

One of the most memorable benefits of Dad's job, at least as far as the Ryan kids were concerned, was the annual Serrick's summer picnic. While the adults hung around in the shade of tall, sprawling oaks drinking beer and eating ham sandwiches, the kids clawed their way through twenty square feet of ankle-deep sawdust that had been salted with nickels. Six-foot-long coolers held free icy-cold bottles of pop in every flavor. Each of us drank as many as possible, because opportunities like this were rare. I always started out with Dodger Wild Cherry, moved on to Dodger Cream Soda, and finished up with a large Coke. By the end of the day, my right arm would be nicely chilled from dipping into the cooler so often.

Of course, no matter how much money Dad earned or wasted, having ten kids was almost guaranteed to keep his family living at the poverty level.

In a single year, ten trips to the dentist, ten new pairs of shoes, and ten piles of school books would put the jackhammer to anyone's bottom line.

Knowing we were poor, however, didn't make my brothers and sisters and me any less happy. In the days before public assistance, Defiance, Ohio, was a good place to grow up in if money was short. The local Lions Club bought our eyeglasses—no small expense for the five of us who needed them. St. Mary's Catholic School waived the annual fees so the Ryans could attend parochial school. Friends and relatives (like Aunt Lucy) were always there to help out.

But the real reason we were a positive-thinking group was our mother, Evelyn Ryan, a woman of high energy and great mirth. Her main creative outlet, aside from having produced the ten of us, was her talent for winning contests. What she called her "knack for words" brought cash and furnishings into the house. In the contest boom years of the forties, fifties, and sixties, magazines and supermarket aisles were filled with product entry blanks, offering big prizes for clever jingles and twenty-five-word-or-less statements on why Dial Soap or Kellogg's Corn Flakes or Heinz Ketchup was the best of its breed. My mother's attention to detail—like noticing that Tootsie Rolls were divided into one-inch segments—was one of the keys to her success. This entry was worth ten dollars:

> For chewy, toothsome, wholesome goodness
> Tootsie Rolls are right—
> Lots of nibbling for a nickel
> And they show me where to bite.

How she found even the time to think clearly in a house with twelve people, most of them under the age of ten, I'll never know. Mom scribbled funny verse and contest entries while ironing, while cooking, while sitting in the back of the church at Sunday Mass. What she didn't find humorous in the world, including her own financial need, could fit into a teacup.

Going, Going, Gone!
We can't take it with us—
That much we all know;
My trouble's been keeping
The stuff 'til I go.

Mom won cars, trips to Europe and New York, TVs, radios, clocks, watches, cameras, bicycles, thousands of dollars in cash, and every appliance we ever owned—from toasters to coffeemakers to blenders to refrigerators. Thanks to our constant financial difficulties, she had to sell the largest prizes to keep the family afloat. Smaller cash prizes were used to pay off medical bills and to spring kids' raincoats and shoes, boys' shirts, and girls' dresses from the limbo of layaway at the local JCPenney store. Beyond the dollar value of all the wins, they instilled in my family a belief in miracles, which buoyed us in hard times.

My mother, five years younger than Dad, was born in 1913, the year Congress imposed federal income taxes. The year Henry Ford pushed the "on" button on the first moving assembly line, and the year a Model T automobile cost four hundred and forty dollars. This was also the year that workers' wages averaged just under three dollars a day, a loaf of bread cost a nickel, a dozen eggs cost a quarter, and a quart of milk cost a dime. A dollar could feed a person for almost a week.

Mom's contest wins brought in a lot of needed money and prizes, but neither her wins nor Dad's weekly paycheck could keep up with leapfrogging expenses. By 1944, after seven years of working at Serrick's machine shop, Dad's take-home pay was $3207.46, just over sixty-one dollars per week. With five children and a wife to support, he must have found it daunting to make ends meet.

In 1954, he would be trying to raise ten children on almost the same pay. Forget making ends meet. Those ends were moving in opposite directions.

Still, the truth is that Kelly Ryan did not enjoy labor—whether he was paid for it or not. He worked at Serrick's from eight to four because he had to. Anything beyond that—mowing the lawn, mending a cracked stair step, fixing a broken lamp—was, to Dad, a useless and falsely pious enterprise.

He liked to take the family for car rides in the countryside when the weather was balmy and the crops were high. We headed out one warm Sunday afternoon, piling into our old blue and white Chevy BelAir, leaving behind appliances in various states of disrepair and a fragile screen door hanging from its frame by a thread. Two blocks from home, Dad spied a middle-aged man raking up leaves from an otherwise pristine lawn and said, in all sincerity, "That sonofabitch thinks he's gonna live forever." He could not fathom personal industry.

Dad also believed that if he had to work for a living, then no other living being should be exempt from the same nine-to-five fate. He envied and despised our cat—a petite black-and-white alley vagrant—and shut her out of the house because, as he often reminded us, "She's too goddamn lazy. All she does is lie around all day." He really meant this. It did no good for one of us to point out that her job was to lie around all day. "The hell with her! Let her work for a living, like I have to, and see how she likes it."

The first house I have any memory of inhabiting was a small, two-bedroom rental on Latty Street, an old and quiet avenue lined with majestic maple trees. The rent came to sixteen dollars a month. My brothers and sisters and I slept in the single upstairs bedroom spread among two double beds and several cots. The house had no bathtub or shower, so those who were young enough to fit took baths in the kitchen sink. My mother washed clothes by hand in an old wringer washer and then dried them on a clothesline suspended between poles leaning at a precarious angle in the back yard. Her work, physical and mental, never stopped.

> Who'd trade
> Peace of mind
> (To most rich men
> Denied)
> For all of their
> Worrisome money?
> I'd.

She knew her life would be a lot easier with an automatic washer and dryer, so she won a set in a 1953 contest. Along with those, she won five thousand dollars in cash, using most of it as a down payment on a four-bedroom house a few blocks away. Four bedrooms and a bathtub! We finally had a home that could accommodate all of us. There was still no privacy (with three kids per bedroom, none of us even had a dresser drawer to call our own), but no one cared.

When, twelve years later, my father secretly took out a four-thousand-dollar second mortgage on the house and couldn't pay the money back to the bank, my mother won another huge contest in the nick of time to save the house from foreclosure.

Thus, over the three decades from 1940 to 1970, our family hop-scotched its way between destitution and deliverance. Some days, we didn't have enough money to pay the milkman; other days, we could have sent him to Europe, all expenses paid.

My parents were apparently destined for financial insecurity—even with no children left at home to support—all the way to the end of their lives. In 1973, at the age of sixty-two, Dad retired after thirty-three years of working at Serrick's. He had been diagnosed with diabetes a few years earlier, but the condition remained manageable as long as he spent a third of the day working and a third of the day sleeping.

Once retired, though, Dad devoted even more hours of the day to drinking, and his circulation slowed to a crawl, causing festering sores on his feet and calves. By this time, Mom worked as a clerk at the JCPenney store and raced back and forth between the Men's Shirts and Pants Department and home, where she tried to heal the leg ulcers with an infusion of aloe vera gel and golden seal.

But in 1974, despite Mom's efforts, one of Dad's legs became gangrenous and had to be amputated. The night after the surgery, the phone rang, and Aunt Lucy, who had kept Mom company at the hospital and driven her home, picked up the receiver. One of the local priests, calling from the hospital, asked to speak to Mom.

"Mrs. Ryan," he said, "we need to know where to bury the leg."

"The leg," Mom repeated. She had no idea what he meant.

"Yes," he said. "Your husband's amputated leg. We need to know what you want done."

"Well, don't you just . . . uh . . . discard it?"

The priest fell silent. Mom, fearing she had said the wrong thing, added, "I mean in some final . . . respectful manner."

"Oh, Mrs. Ryan," he said. "No. It's a Catholic leg and has to be buried in consecrated ground. You understand."

But Mom, who was raised Methodist and converted to Catholicism only when she married Dad, didn't understand. "Consecrated ground?" she said. "You mean like a cemetery plot?"

"Well, not a whole plot, necessarily, but in a portion of a plot in the Catholic section of the cemetery."

Mom could see the dollar signs adding up. "Egad, Father, you mean a full burial? With a casket? With a headstone?"

"No, no, no, Mrs. Ryan," he said. "That's not necessary. Don't you already have a plot at Riverside?"

"Well . . . no," Mom said. An expense like that was the least of her worries. "I guess Kelly and I have been too busy paying off the debts we've accumulated while alive. I'm sorry, Father, you've got me flustered. I'm afraid I'll have to think about this and call you back."

Then Lucy, who had overheard Mom's half of the conversation and immediately guessed Father's half, laughed and said, "Oh heck, Evelyn, just toss it in my plot."

And so they did. With requisite ceremony and little expense, a small but deep hole was dug in a corner of Lucy Agnes Moore's personal plot in Riverside Cemetery in Defiance, Ohio, and the remains were interred.

Aunt Lucy died in 1989 and was buried in the same plot as her brother's leg. Dad died in 1983, and was buried in a plot the Ryans were eventually able to afford. Mom died in 1998. Evelyn and Kelly Ryan rest side by side in the cemetery, about ten yards west of Dad's Catholic leg.

MY FATHER'S HANDS

Daisy Hernández

My father is in his sixties. He is a tall, thin man with an almost bald head. He has a small beer belly beneath his white cotton T-shirt. His hands are never empty. There is always a cigar, cigarette, or beer can in them. He's handsome, and he's an alcoholic.

Years before the Cuban revolution, my father, then a teenager, saw a soldier in the hills where he and his family picked coffee beans, cut sugar cane, and raised pigs. He liked the soldier's matching jacket and pants, the uniform's sense of purpose. My father didn't want to be a farmer. He wanted something more. He wanted to be on the side that won.

Some years later, he got the uniform and fought against Fidel Castro. Unfortunately, he only talks about it now when he's drunk, slurring the words and his history into a number of possibilities. But this much is true, he says: It isn't easy to switch sides in a war. So he left the island along with the United States embassy workers and came to New Jersey, where he cut hair, opened a bakery, painted houses, closed the bakery, and cut wood. By the early 1970s, he had settled into factory work and married my Colombian mother.

He returned to visit Cuba once before NAFTA and told his cousins how good work was in the north. His job was to stay up through the night with a textile machine. He'd replace needles that broke and alert the bosses to any problems. It was he and the night and the deafening sound of the machines. He didn't need more than a few English phrases. On weekends he made extra money helping with plumbing, electricity—those many jobs where a man is always useful.

Then, in the nineties, factories began closing. My father's work hours were cut from twelve a day to eight, and then six. I began finding him home at all hours of the day and night and after awhile I stopped asking why, because all he would say was, "*Se terminó el trabajo* (the work ended)." The work ended like a novel, its mournful last page close at hand.

When he wasn't on the clock, my father drank. His hands would point at me and remind me to study hard because "you don't want to end up at a factory like your mother and me." Even before I understood words and phrases like "manual labor," "working class," and "alcoholism," I knew how they felt: like my father's hands.

Parts of my father's hands are dead. The skin has protected itself by hardening, turning his large hands into a terrain of calluses and scars, the deep lines scattered on his palms like dirt roads that never intersect. His hands are about power and survival, my first lessons about class. The dreaded question comes on Wednesday afternoons when my father drags the trash cans to the curb. That's when the Colombian lady across the street pushes her screen door open. She's noticed my father at home lately and asks him about his job. When he tells her the factory is closed *por ahora*, she tilts her head like she already knew. "*Y estás colectando?*"

What she really wants to know is if he's collecting unemployment benefits.

"There's no work to be found," my father answers. His pants are falling from his narrow hips and he yanks them up with his left hand.

"*Pero, estás colectando?*"

My father shrugs his shoulders. "*Es la mísma basura.*" It's the same garbage.

He wishes the Colombian lady well. From my bedroom window, I watch him walk into the two-family house he and my mother bought with years of savings. In the basement, he finishes a six-pack of Coors beer and listens to Radio WADO. He's found a store down Bergenline Avenue where the price of beer drops when unemployment rises.

At Catholic Mass on Sunday, the collection basket makes the rounds. The Cold War is over, but the world is still divided into good and evil, democracy and communism, Catholics and others, the ones who give and the ones who collect. It is a simple arrangement. One ill-spoken word could damn you to hell, communism, and poverty.

There is some comfort in knowing even God has to collect. But still the church's collection basket makes me anxious. I'm afraid we don't have money to give because, when it comes to Strawberry Shortcake stickers, my mother says we don't have the money. In church, my eyes rarely turn to her. Instead, I listen carefully to hear whether her pocketbook will join the others to interrupt the church's silence. It does.

The collection baskets crawl down each pew and swallow the sounds of crinkled dollars and jingling coins. I hold two, sometimes four quarters, excited to throw them into the basket. The tap dancing of those coins into the basket makes me feel we are as good as any of the families here with five-dollar bills in their hands.

Spanish is a Romance language except when you're trying to make ends meet. The Spanish we speak is a language in which life is reduced to talking about what you need, what's working and what isn't. *No hay trabajo. Media libra de chuletas. Basta ya. Van pal'iglesia. Estás colectando?*

Are you collecting? The rest of that sentence, the words "unemployment benefits," never makes it into Spanish. There is no need for it, because everyone here knows what is meant when the question is asked. No one says we're "receiving" or "getting," because no one here really believes we have a right to that money. You're "collecting" because you don't have work. You're one step away from *la gente en* welfare and two steps away from the old lady at Port Authority who's collecting pennies from commuters. Even in English, we call it "unemployment *benefits*," thinking it's a benefit to get something back from the work we do.

I live with Spanish, with coming home to find my mother watching a *telenovela*. Her factory shut down for a few days and her Spanish words are to the point. "Your father's in the basement. They called from work, said to not come today."

In the basement, my father talks to Elegua, an Afro-Cuban god without hands who lives in a clay dish and opens doors. He has only a face, sculpted into a round pointy crown. When my father is collecting unemployment, he feeds Elegua more candy and espresso so the god will open the door to another job.

Elegua is better than learning English. He's the god of trickery and journeys; you can trust him more than English words that change tenses, don't sound the way they look, and get turned on you at the factory.

As a child, I am drawn to Elegua and his candy dish. The Cuban women explain to my Colombian mother that Elegua loves children and that's why I'm spending time with him. But they are wrong. I am a practical child. Elegua's the god who opens doors and I am desperately trying to get away from my father's angry, drunk hands, and the feeling that our destinies are scribbled in the square opaque windows of my father's factory. Because Elegua is the god of crossroads, I imagine he understands the contradiction of my growing up: that I want to escape from my father and also take him with me, that I want to flee my life without leaving Papi behind.

I am meant to escape. Everyone tells me so at the barbecue for my mother's birthday. "Girl, you're going to be something some day. You're going to make it. Irma, will you look at this thing the *nena* wrote for the school paper, her name and everything. Girl, you're going places." No one ever says where I am going, but they are sure that a place is waiting for me.

By the time I am nine and translating my report card for my father, I know he is not going with me.

In elementary school, I hear that Americans are trying to keep up with a family named Joneses. The Joneses are a mystery of the English language. My mother says she's never heard of *"la família Yoneses"* and I should quit worrying about what everybody else is doing.

In our part of the world, no one is keeping up. We belong to a community based on the fact that we are all doing bad. When someone does a little better, there is an unspoken betrayal. You smile at them and when they leave, you talk about how they are lying to get welfare checks, working *por la izquierda,* putting on airs. When you are the one doing better, you sit at your kitchen table and say, "It's incredible but true. Any little good thing you got, somebody else wants." You talk about how *celoso,* jealous, people can be. It is easier to say that people are jealous than admit they have a right to want something better.

It takes years for me to understand that the Joneses happen only in English, in houses where people cook in one room and eat in another. The Joneses don't happen where people are called "white trash" and "spics," "welfare queens" and "illegals." And no one ever asks the Joneses if they are collecting.

When someone asks my father how he is doing, he looks at his hands, studies the scattering of black scars and the dryness of the skin. His answer is always the same, *"Ahí, caballero, en la misma lucha."*

When I ask him what it means to say you are in the same *lucha,* my father says it means you are doing the same old thing. Years later in community activism, that's all I hear, that we're in this *lucha* together. *Lucha* means struggle, someone tells me. The same old thing, *la lucha.* I sit at a lesbian collective meeting, my hand clasping my pen tightly. It's hard to explain how in one moment, someone can translate a word and your understanding of your family and your history can be turned around.

In the mid-nineties, the *lucha* changed. Neighbors began talking about working as home attendants. The closed factories began outnumbering the ones that stayed open, and the new jobs were in cleaning floors and baby diapers and serving food. Men from Central America arrived, renting the first floor of our home, eight men, two bedrooms. The whites who could moved out. People came from all parts: Mexico, Pakistan, Brazil, India. The men waited at the street corner for construction work that barreled down the street in blue pickup trucks. In our basement, the Spanish newspaper was marked in red ink with circles and X's.

My father survived the onset of NAFTA because of the Cuban revolution. A political refugee, he was entitled to citizenship and the unemployment benefits that carried us between his jobs. The newer immigrants and those who came from other countries didn't have his privileges.

At the unemployment agency, he sat alongside African Americans, Pakistanis, Dominicans, and Nigerians, and they learned the English words for the work they did, and how to spell them. "Embroidery." "Seamstress." "Machine operator."

Factories closed for a week, a month, forever, and we waited for the phone to ring. The calls came randomly. At first the voices were Pure American English, a language that rarely falters. It begins with a "hey, your dad home?" and ends with a "thanks."

I was never to say that my father was out looking for another job or that he'd found one, part-time. I was never to reveal anything over the phone. Just take the message.

Sometimes the factory had not closed but "tell your dad to come at eight, not five, tonight." Or, "Tell him we need him tonight." "Tell him to call us next week." "Tell him he can file for unemployment."

As the years passed, the factories changed hands and the callers changed. The American voices disappeared and were replaced by an English that stumbled all over itself. "Halo, Ignacio?" No, he's not home. "Eh, tell him, no work, eh, come ehere efriday."

Even the unemployment agency changed to a new dial-in system to collect unemployment benefits. The brochure came in Spanish and English.

My mother studied it carefully. My father made the money and my mother handled it. She wrote the checks, paid the bills, and completed the forms for unemployment with me. My father's hands could do many things, but handling money was not one of them. Making phone calls was not one of them, either. His hands would wake me up with a gentle shake. He'd still be sober. "Your mother called unemployment and couldn't get through. Come on, get up, call them."

The dial-in system was fabulously efficient. Much more so than the factories that closed.

If your social security number ends on an odd number, call on Tuesday. If it ends on an even number, call on Thursday. Enter the weeks for which you're claiming.

The dial-in system was clever. They said it was to help us, to avoid waiting at the agency for a long time. I suspect it was the best way to handle a possible riot as the economy switched from the manufacturing to the service sector. Not making a trip to the agency meant you wouldn't have to see in one room how many other people were going through the same thing. When you did show up (because the phone system didn't work), there were fewer people, even though back on your street you knew it was more people than that. You began to doubt yourself. Maybe it wasn't so bad.

Not going to the agency meant you could avoid seeing the pain of other people. You didn't need to know English to understand the agency man telling someone on the line that "no, sir, according to this you have nothing left to collect." You didn't need a translation for the immigrant man's English words, "But I no find job." And then came that dreaded English word—"welfare." "Sir, I'm gonna need for you to get off this line because we can't help you here. Get on the line at window four and you can talk to someone there about welfare."

Calling in, you could avoid that man's eyes, the way his brown body, sheltered under five layers of clothes against the winter storm, turned away and left. You could avoid looking at his empty hands. You could avoid thinking about what would happen one day when none of us could collect.

The only thing I feared more than my father not being able to collect was time spent collecting. At least when there was work he wasn't around drinking and yelling at me as much. The world was cruel to him, yes, but it was hard for me to be angry and afraid of an abstract idea like "world." It was easier to be afraid of my father's hands. Easier to be angry when the blistered and swaying drunk hands slapped me on the back of my head. And there were other emotions that came more easily than anger: fear and guilt. Fear that life would always be like this—at the mercy of a factory closing, a paycheck arriving. Guilt because I—with my English words and schooling—would one day lead a different life than his. I just had to get there.

For about a year, I worked at McDonald's. I worked the register and got free meals. My job meant that if I set my mind to it and flirted with the right managers, I could become a manager too, with paid vacation, paid sick time, and a steady paycheck. So I watched my classmates play softball, run for student council, and drive their new Nissans. I'd get home and change from my Catholic uniform to my McD's one. If I worked enough hours, I made as much as my mother did at the factory.

On Saturdays, the manager created competitions to make us work faster. "The register that makes the most money before noon gets two tickets to Loews movie theater!" It was the first time anyone had ever referred to me as a machine. But I just smiled politely. I was proud of learning the register, its grid of prices. Big Macs, Large Fries, Apple Pies. But the manager was right. In a matter of months, I had become a machine. You had to shut down some part of yourself to the sexist jokes, to your hours cut when a new manager took over the schedules and didn't like you. The job was like walking on a tightrope without a net. You are up in the air alone. Interacting with other people is an act of acrobatics. You never know who will start talking shit about you. You never know what will piss off your boss. You never know why they sent you home but not the others. A wrong word could mean your hours the next week were reduced from forty to thirty-two.

It's hard to write this part of the story. It's the part of the story I never talk about with my New York friends, writer friends, community activist friends, with anyone. We act the same—like we never worked with our hands. Sometimes we mention in conversation that we worked menial jobs, we stripped, we waited tables, we worked fast-food jobs, we cleaned diapers. We use those middle-class words to describe experiences that are not middle-class. But we don't know how else to talk about them.

It's hard to write about how quickly I moved that Saturday, how jealous and ashamed I was when I came in a close second for those tickets. It's hard to write about burning my fingers at the fry machine, how the grease of the place sticks to your skin, how you take the money you earn to the nail salon and get long acrylic tips and for a moment forget you are at a job that slowly turns your hands to cardboard. And it's harder still to know that a good number of people don't work and live like this. Harder still to know those people are your teachers, your friends who live in towns where McDonald's aren't even allowed to open.

In college and after, there are other jobs, the ones you really talk about over dinner with friends. The job at the library, the newspaper, the publishing house. But after years of numbing myself to working-class life, an alcoholic father, a fast-food job, it isn't easy to make myself feel something. I am too used to a world where trips to museums are something you do on class trips in high school. Our passions weren't work, but what we saw on the Spanish news, our romantic lives, losing weight, getting pregnant, waiting to love, wanting to be loved, the specials on Bergenline, the freebies at the Macy's Clinique counter with a purchase of $19.95. We talked about dreams, where we'd go if we had all the money in the world, who we would marry if we could pick anyone.

Those office jobs after college meant walking into a place where people didn't dream like that. They had jobs they liked, money-market accounts, paid vacation time. Dreams were something that actually happened. No one talked about buying a Lotto ticket.

More than anything now I am trying to feel something rather than numbing myself to the gap between my father and me, between the past and the present. I get a paycheck for writing newspaper articles about unemployment, while he works part-time as a janitor. Friends tell me to feel accomplished, that my résumé is a reflection of him, his sacrifices and triumphs. That's probably true, but it doesn't resonate.

The only things that do make me feel something are art, writing about him, loving him, taking pictures of his hands, listening to him tell me I should photograph this one scar on his index finger. He can't remember how he got it.

WINTER COAT

Terri Griffith

"Do you get enough to eat at home?" the school nurse asks, as she sets the clipboard in her lap and looks at me earnestly.

"Yeah," I answer, not really sure what she's getting at.

"Did your mom make you dinner last night?"

"Yeah."

"What did she make?"

"Macaroni and cheese."

"Did you have breakfast this morning?"

"Uh-huh."

"Do you have breakfast every morning?"

I don't know why the nurse is asking me these questions. I don't know why she came to my classroom and in front of my classmates asked Mr. Logan to have me excused. But it's obvious from the sound of her voice and her overly controlled tone that she thinks my mom has done something wrong. Maybe it's me who's done something wrong. Her questions make no sense. How can I give her the right answer if I can't understand why she's asking me these things? I don't want to get my mom in trouble. She wants to know what my mom feeds me. Maybe my mom cooks the wrong food. Maybe I eat the wrong things. Maybe it's because I didn't finish my vegetables last night.

"Well, I'm concerned because you're underweight. You're very small for your age."

The nurse was right about that. When I was in elementary school, I was small for my age, but it wasn't because I didn't eat. I ate fine, in a '70s sort of way. Beanie Weenie. Meatloaf with corn. Frozen fried chicken with salad. I never once went hungry. But there were a lot of times when I complained and didn't finish my dinner, especially after the third night of split-pea soup with ham hocks and carrots. Now, when I look back on the times when I think I might have gone hungry, my mom and I conveniently went to dinner at her best friend's house. For a while, we ate dinner at her house a lot.

Just four years later, in the sixth grade, I would be the second-tallest girl in the class, complete with boobs and a period. I was never the skinniest girl in my grade; Sarah was. Her parents were rich. I bet no one pulled Sarah from class to ask her what she had for dinner last night.

When I started kindergarten, not one of my classmates had parents who were divorced; I was the only one. But by the time I was in junior high, more than half the class came from single-parent homes. Without exception, all of us kids were raised by our mothers, who worked two, sometimes three jobs to support their families. It was just my mom and me, and although things seemed bad, other families had it much worse than we did.

The 1980s were hard on the Pacific Northwest economy. Many people lost their jobs, the timber industry collapsed, lumber mills closed, the salmon runs were depleted. The families in my neighborhood were all tied to these economies—families I considered rich because the kids played on soccer teams, bought their school clothes at department stores, and lived in houses their parents owned. Now I understand that these families weren't rich at all. Their fathers were longshoremen, their mothers worked at the paper mill, their family owned a fishing boat. All of these people had working-class jobs, hard jobs that extract the life from a person. I guess I was lucky when I was young—my mom had a white-collar job working for the Department of Corrections. Even though it sounds fancy, it didn't pay much—but she made ends meet. Then my mom got laid off, and life for us got much harder.

The thing about being poor is that you know what it means to be poor—and there's always someone poorer than you. For all my funky hand-me-down clothes from my mom's best friend's children, there was always some girl in class with greasy hair who smelled like pee and didn't have a winter coat.

My school didn't make it any easier to be poor, though at first glance it might have seemed as if it did. We "free lunch" kids stood in a separate line and had to give our names to the Lunch Lady, who checked us off her list. For what? To make sure we didn't get two lunches? The Lunch Lady said we had to stand in this "special" line so that she could keep track of which kids "took advantage" of their free lunch. It always felt as if we stood in that line to make sure there was no confusion between whose parents could pay for a hot lunch and whose couldn't.

The really poor kids got free breakfast, too. This was the worst of all possible elementary school fates—being tagged "free breakfast." When my mom told me that I was to leave the house a half hour early so that I could have breakfast in the cafeteria, I nearly died. I didn't want to go, didn't want to face the other kids I would be joining. Their parents didn't have jobs, they came from huge families, and at least a fourth of them were from the giant government-run Children's Center, two blocks away.

These Children's Center kids had, as the principal described in a special assembly (without them), "behavioral problems," and weren't able to stay in regular foster homes with real families like other boys and girls. Back then I didn't know who those kids were. I do now. Who's labeled "incorrigible" at six? What kind of fourth-grader is unplaceable in foster care? Kids who are abused sexually and physically, kids who are drug-addicted at birth, that's who.

I was terrified of what these children might do to me. They were animals—we had been warned. Would they beat me up? Stab me in the leg with a fork? I would be one of these "free-breakfast" kids, and now everyone would know it.

At first, I simply didn't go to school early. I took my time, played in the gully, sat in the alley outside my best friend's house until she left out the back door so we could walk to school together. I waited out the breakfast portion of my day, but I was a little girl and I got hungry. Free, hot breakfast was waiting for me if I were willing to claim it.

The free breakfast my school provided was too tempting to resist. Pancakes, syrup, bacon. Scrambled eggs, sausage, cinnamon rolls. My mother's idea of a yummy breakfast consisted of bland puffed rice, dreary puffed corn, and the narcotic winter favorite, Cream of Wheat with a square of melty margarine on top. Of course, I gave in. Even so, I still had my pride. I wasn't about to give up my breakfast secret that easily. My technique was this—I shoveled the hot breakfast into my mouth as fast as possible, then shot my hand into the air and waited as the lunchroom attendant came and checked my plate to make sure I'd eaten every bite. If I ate fast enough, I could make it out of the cafeteria and into the hallway before the regular kids started arriving. That way, everyone would think I was just an early riser and not the "free breakfast" I really was.

"Cops are gone," Ricky yells from the top of the stairs.

Who knows how long we have been in that basement room, all thirty of us, crowded together, waiting in the dark, the only sound that of someone taking a slurp from their beer can. It happens all the time. The band is playing upstairs, someone spots a cop car, and we all rush to the basement before they make it to the front door. The band members always stay upstairs and pretend it is an innocent band practice that is making all the noise.

"No, officer, there isn't anyone else here. Just us." Then Ricky mumbles some promises of a quieter rehearsal, and the cops leave.

I head back upstairs to look for Kelly, a girl I can't quite call my girlfriend because we are both closeted and we only ever kiss when we both get drunk enough to make out in a back room or some car, anyplace our boyfriends won't catch us.

The two of us talk about music, smoke cigarettes, discuss what edgy book we've just read, drink even more beer, and make plans to see whatever cool band is playing in Seattle next weekend. What we never talk about is our future, what college we will go to, what we want to do for a living, what we want to be when we grow up. From where we stand, it is impossible to see our way out. We keep our talk simple. Even if we do harbor secret hopes for what our lives might someday be, we don't share them. I know it is foolish to think I can climb my way out of this ditch and into the American Dream. Eventually, Kelly will stumble back behind her drum kit and the band will start playing again (a little softer this time), until the early hours of the morning.

It's hard to plan for the future when there isn't one. What did the world have to offer us working-class kids? In the eighties, if you had money, or thought you might ever have money, you were preppy: applied to business school, liked Michael J. Fox, read books by Bret Easton Ellis. If you didn't have money and never expected to, you joined a band, went to shows on the weekend, drank cheap beer, and listened to hardcore.

With few exceptions, none of us were bad kids. Well . . . sometimes we behaved badly, but there was never malicious intent. My friends moved into "the city" (population 75,000), where I lived. They came from rural areas, towns with 5,000 people, the neighboring islands, and the reservation. A bunch of scruffy punk rockers who worked as cooks, like me, or at the lumberyard or shake mill. For some of my friends, life didn't turn out too well. Many of us ended up strung out, in prison, or dead. Some got permanent work at the paper mill or airplane factory. Others became teachers, professional musicians, and parents.

What's a young dyke with no role models to do? How could I conceptualize a future that I had never seen? I had met a couple of grown-up lesbians before. There was Butch, who worked at our neighborhood gas station. I never thought much about it, just figured she was another girl with a boy's name, like Sam or Pat or Stevie. It wasn't until high school that I realized "Butch" was probably not the name her mother gave her. Then there were the ladies who worked at the paper mill. Flannel shirts and shift work, that's what I thought being a lesbian meant. I couldn't be a lesbian; I wasn't anything like those women.

My mom raised me to be middle management, to go to college—community college first, then state college (scholarship willing). I was specifically brought up to not go to work at our town's ubiquitous factories. Pink collar over blue collar any day! I was also raised to not take risks, not because my mother thought I was incapable of taking care of myself, but because she believed that a steady paycheck was the key to a happy life, which it just might be. My mom wanted my future to contain all the things she didn't have. New clothes, the ability to pay the electric bill when it was due, the luxury of hoping to someday own my own home.

Without the protection economic stability provides, there is no room for failure. I had no room to fail. My mother had no room to fail. When a child is raised to always take the safe road, the intention is to make that child's life easier, to empower her with financial security. But really, it only teaches her that she can't do anything.

I stood on the train this morning wearing my new winter coat. I live in Chicago now, and it's the coldest place I have ever been, below-zero cold, cold that can kill you. The kind of coat you wear tells everyone on the train who you are. She's poor: She's wearing two lightweight coats that look like they came from a thrift store, or "resale shop," as they're called here. He's rich: His coat is black leather and lined with fur. She's working class: Her coat is warm and puffy, but a few years old and machine washable. In Chicago your coat is a statement of your material worth. You don't really think the stars of hip-hop videos wear those down-filled or shearling coats because they're cold, do you? Before I moved to Chicago, coats didn't mean anything to me.

Chicago has poor like I didn't even know existed—public housing projects that go on, literally, for miles; families of six living in one-bedroom apartments and people sleeping under the elevated train tracks. And there's rich like I've never seen, except on television—women and men wearing full-length furs on the street, three-hundred-dollar dinners for two, and eight-million-dollar condominiums. Oprah lives here!

My new coat cost two hundred dollars. I've never spent that much money on an article of clothing in my life—not shoes, not even a bridesmaid's dress. My coat is black wool, with shiny buttons. It's fitted, long, and has an opulent black fox collar and cuffs. I wear this coat to job interviews, out to dinner, and sometimes to parties. I will not wear this coat to bars or shows, anywhere I think will be too smoky or where someone might slop beer on it or burn me with a cigarette. This coat will be expensive to clean.

Despite its warmth and evident beauty, my coat makes me uncomfortable. I have never owned a coat so nice and I am afraid the other passengers know this too. I look around the train to see if anyone is looking at me. In this coat, I feel like a spectacle.

What do people think of me? Do they think I'm rich? Am I rich? I bought this coat, even though it was with a credit card. I'm scared to wear it too much because I don't want to wreck it, or wear it out, or spill something on it. My girlfriend says, "Wear the coat! It's not made of gold," though to me it is. Can the people on the train tell that I am ill at ease in something so costly? Do they think I am trying to pass for something I am not? Am I trying to pass? I worry most about what the working-class people on the train think. I want to go up to everyone wearing a faded old coat and say, "My clothes, what I have on underneath, all of it comes from the Salvation Army! Really, this is a fluke. Really, I am one of you." I don't say these things, but I think them.

Is this what growing up "without" means—that I can (almost) afford a fancy coat, but can't enjoy it? What about the American Dream, the theory that with hard work and perseverance people can transcend the class into which they are born? I want to believe in it, but I don't. Class is about more than money; it's about safety and security, knowing that what you have today, you will have tomorrow. It's about having faith and feeling safe in the knowledge that when my coat gets worn out, there will be other coats.

When I get home from work, I place my new coat on a wooden hanger, and hang it on the shower-curtain rod. I do up all the buttons, smooth it out, then go over it with a lint brush. I am going to make this coat last forever.

THE JUST-ADD-WATER KENNEDYS AND BARBECUE BREAD VIOLENCE

Polyestra

Fewer than one percent of Americans break out of the class they are born into. Despite these grim odds, people like my parents still base their entire lives on the dream of class jumping. The television gospel told them it was not only possible, but normal. To not increase your wealth was more shameful, to my family, than a brown lawn, unusual offspring, and unemployment combined. They considered every day that went by without a yacht and a swimming pool embarrassing. And everyone else in the neighborhood who didn't miraculously obtain a new Cadillac or a vacation home at the beach, or who was still working construction or driving a cab, was equally shameful. To my parents, every day in this working-class neighborhood was temporary. It was just a matter of working hard enough.

My parents didn't think of "class" as an ingrained culture, as a part of who they were. They had no pride in where they came from, only in where they dreamed of going. They were two out of millions who erased themselves for the homogeneity of TV-inspired blandness, smiling into cereal commercials like adoring fans. The American Dream. Television was a sick ritual for people like my parents. After dinner my father would peel down to his undershirt and light up a cigar, clenching it between his lead- and mercury-filled molars (some strange side effect of serving in the military). He reclined in his personal chair, his oiled black pompadour shining in the TV's light. My mother perched posture-perfectly on the sinking couch. They pored over images of gluttonous mansions and commented on how they would arrange the furniture in such a place, what color scheme they would apply to each room, where to put the remote control, rotating fireplace, and wishing fountain. They wanted every car in every car ad, every diamond ring, dinette set, wide-screen television. Their idea of "rich" wasn't being able to afford furniture from somewhere other than Sears, but being able to afford the most expensive furniture, and a lot of it, from Sears.

Every weekend we went to my grandparents' house, no skipping allowed. If we were all dying of pneumonia, we were still required to go, or suffer the wrath of Thelma and Johnny. My father's parents were hardcore about their son becoming a millionaire. They had been through the Depression. Their lives reeked of financial failure and poverty—one big drag for all the world to know about—and now it was up to my father to save them from dying in shame. These were bitter people: The old man chain-smoked and drank canned beer while the woman actually wept over "the mixing of the races." They had been robbed and screwed over, or had screwed themselves over, so many times they had developed a fear of hordes of non-Caucasians entering their row house at night to kill them and make off with their nicotine-stained divan, their silver utensils (which were hidden in the wall of the cellar), their rechargeable electric grass clippers, their monogrammed pen and notepad set from 1939. Even in the worst dry spell of generic-cigarette half-price sales, their son would surely save them. Even if they ran out of green olives for their "special occasion" martinis, even if the TV went on the fritz during *The Lawrence Welk Show*, my father would save them. Even if my grandfather slipped away into an alternate plane, humming songs of Austria while belching up bile and swallowing it again, which he did, my father would take care of them. And so he did.

My parents had two kids, both of whose purpose in life was to become rich. The torch had been passed. It was now my parents' goal to mold us into something "rich," to strategically insert us into the upper crust, thus ensuring a wealthy retirement. Their first attempt at this was to enroll my sister and me in private school (from which we were rapidly ejected, since they couldn't pay for it). They insisted this would give my sister and me a much better chance of marrying some sweaty-palmed old-money boy when the time came. Unfortunately, they overlooked the fact that these rich children wanted nothing to do with us. The rich, like those mysterious Masons and the CIA, have seriously tight-ass circles that not just anyone can penetrate. This really messed with my sister's mind; she was in a constant state of agony. All the other girls in her classes had designer jeans, and my sister was the only one in the whole school suffering without. My mother sewed fake patches onto generic jeans, but this only made the whole thing worse when a classmate ratted her out.

Next they enrolled my sister and me in ballroom-dancing classes at the country club, where we were nearly guaranteed to become "cultured" and "civilized." This move was in part a response to my natural attraction to vandalism and dirt-bike ganging, which severely infringed upon my parents' princess dreams. At the country club, they thought, we would learn how to charm the hell out of the rich, play their games, rub elbows with the next generation of money people. Membership was by invitation only. We were the only kids in the classes whose parents weren't members. These kids came from well-known, old-money families. For them, the waltz and the fox trot were some sort of perverse "fun," where they got dressed up and twirled around a ballroom like royalty. To me, it was horror.

Everything about me showed I didn't belong, from my inappropriate, not-quite-formal tube dresses to my macramé jewelry. (Our clothing arrived in the mail from our Canadian cousins—hand-me-downs from the hinterland—and was better suited to square dancing and getting beat up in a big city.) My mother tried to compensate by hand-sewing me the gaudiest satin and lace dresses. She went for the latest fad: low-waisted, poofed-out dresses that made me look like my torso was twice as long as my legs, like some shapeless, disproportionate mutant. She even bought me little white gloves—like the JonBenet freakazoids wear on the creepy children's talent shows in Atlantic City—and patent-leather Mary Janes.

Once a week, my mother, in her beige polyester London Fog–style overcoat and metallic-blue eye shadow, her helmet perm and beige secretary pumps, drove me up the winding road of manicured grounds in our clunking Toronado station wagon. At the top of the hill sat the Colonial castle within which waited the liverwurst-scented old ladies with castanets and the teeming brood of the stinking rich of Delaware, all prissied up like miniature millionaires. There I slouched in a "period" chair against the wall while all the little boys in suits and gloves chose all the little girls in velvet and lace, leaving me to sit there for the entire time. One of the deeply creased, too-much-sun-in-a-lifetime old ladies sometimes forced one of the boys to dance with me—more as a punishment to some lazy boy than to help me. Their parents were Du Ponts and oil tycoons, and one boy, his rubbery hand like a hoof on my hip, said to me, "You'll never marry one of us."

"I know," I said, and I wasn't offended. I had gone to private school with this arrogant little boy, who was commonly known as "Booger" for his ever-sunken finger in his ape-shaped right nostril. I just wanted to go ride my bike down a steep, rocky embankment, give someone a black eye. Instead I found myself seated at a very long table, my eyes full of what seemed like hundreds of sparkling utensils. We were "quizzed" during each course of a sickeningly massive meal as to which utensil to use. My hand trembled over the fourth fork from the left, the knife located beside the smallest plate, expecting a slap on the wrist from one of the wrinkled mummies. Each item presented by some annoyed waiter was smothered in hollandaise. Boiled meat and hollandaise. String beans and hollandaise. All this in preparation for a final banquet and ball, to which the parents were invited to get loaded and watch their kids do the bunny hop. I was thankful to find out we weren't invited, but my sister wept bitter tears for days. Her sorrow worsened when we found out we were the only ones enrolled in the classes who weren't invited. My parents complained that they hadn't gotten their money's worth for the classes. They couldn't understand what had gone wrong.

My mother worked at a bank with Bruce Willis's mom. Every day, sucking up minimum wage, my mom told Bruce Willis's mom about how she would be rich someday. My father worked at Sears with Elvis Presley's drummer. He did the same. He asked a customer, "You want us to rotate the tires while we're at it?" and then told Elvis Presley's drummer how he would be rich someday. Elvis Presley's drummer rotated the tires, smiled slowly at my dad, and went to the bar after work like everyone else. The reality of working shit jobs somehow didn't sway them from their delusion. Instead of resenting the rich, who would never let them into their club, they talked about them as if they were family: "George Wellingham III got a new Porsche!" "Ivana Porkroll is divorcing Richard—it will split the families for sure." "Little Rutherford Hoggerton has been chosen to go to the military academy—did you hear, girls? He's your age!"

Every day when I walked to school I walked past the private school, where my friends and I were harassed by a bunch of horse-faced blondes in team shorts, holding on to lacrosse sticks. It just so happened that the school had constructed a pedestrian tunnel under the road, and a few kids from our school had been killed crossing the street there, so we opted to walk through the tunnel. "No white trash allowed!" they would bellow, threatening to call the cops. The property between the private school and the public school was all Du Pont estates. One day an old lady in the back of a limo pulled up next to us on the street and told us she didn't want us walking past her driveway—on the public street. She wrote down our names and said she would notify the authorities of our intentions to rob the Du Ponts. My associates and I decorated the walls of the tunnel with slogans, such as, Rich Fucks, Fucking Snobs, Eat Shit Moneybags.

My father quit Sears and plunged headlong into sales. Real estate. He worked seven-day weeks for the same or less pay than the Sears job. It seemed like a turn for the worse, but then, rather suddenly, my father started making money. A lot of money. They went on vacations to the Caribbean (a perk from the company for high sales), from which they returned with rolls of photos of dangerously sunburned, severely inebriated Realtors and their spouses, their heads wrapped in wet towels, their swollen faces sucking on mixed drinks; dance floors full of drunken, Delawarean Realtors screaming into the dirt under a limbo bar; Realtor wives shielding their eyes from the camera while Realtor husbands bend them over folding chairs for a mimicked spanking.

My parents gave in to the reality of their long-awaited fantasy. They bought stuff like crazy. They bought rental properties and a beach house, new cars, an antique car. They hired a maid. They bought my sister and me jewelry and clothing, furniture and toys, new everything they could get their hands on. The hand-me-down hoe-down clothes were quickly replaced by rich-kid fashion, which sent me into a junior-high identity crisis. For the first time I realized I was trapped between classes—considered too uppity by the poorer kids, and having nothing in common, except the same uniform, with the richer kids. I sat alone in my suddenly made-over bedroom, stripped of its chaotic wall of Scratch-n-Sniff stickers, Scott Baio and *Dukes of Hazzard* posters, and giant carnival-prize stuffed animals. My completely whitewashed new room, with custom-designed cabinets, framed fine art posters, and a vanity full of gold jewelry and make-up, was completely foreign and frightening. I hid the jewelry, afraid it would be stolen and my parents would never forgive me.

Now we were going to brunch at ritzy hotels, driving to Pennsylvania to try the latest new fancy restaurant. It was all an abrupt turn from my mother's infamous boiled-chicken dinner. It seemed like one night we were carefully removing the nearly liquid white skin from a boiled chicken leg, swallowing half a softer-than-butter boiled onion—and the next night our dinner was being served on fire. My father, who was almost always embarrassingly drunk and loud at such occasions, was glaringly out of place in his red suit and American flag/bald eagle tie, using a long umbrella with the head of a duck as a cane, his lips pulled back in a huge, unconvincing smile, framing half an unlit cigar in his teeth. Yet there I sat, in some hideous pastel dress and flats, watching the waiter's mouth as he asked us to quiet down/put out that cigar/pay the tab and leave.

At home in our big house flanked by new cars and gaudy decoration, our better-than-thou-neighbors' posturing was scandalously tarnished by barbecue bread violence. My father insisted on a loaf of bread being present at meals, to save him from choking (some weird thing from my grandmother). During the summer we usually ate outside on our deck, which was highly visible to the entire neighborhood. By the end of the meal, my drunk-ass dad would almost always be ready for a fight—any fight—and he usually let loose on the bag of bread first. Neighbors would stare shamelessly as my father pitched the loaf into the chain-link fence, where it would explode into a tragedy of misshapen slices while he bellowed, "I bring home the bread!" This popular exclamation was heard by all on many occasions from my father: from the second-floor balcony in his underwear, from the lawn with shotguns in each hand, from his car wrestling with my mother for the keys.

Their dream for us hadn't died. Higher education, to my parents, was still a way for their children to jump class. And so, when the time came, they insisted we go to college, though both of us protested. We would be the first in both of their families to go. They were sure that with our first step on campus we would meet scads of tall, block-jawed future doctors and lawyers who would fall in love with our cultured, high-class charm as soon as they laid eyes on us. My sister's Mohawk and chain-smoking of menthol 100s, and my common pastime of watching TV flat on my back with a bowl of cereal propped between my breasts, somehow didn't dissolve their mirage. These were just phases that would end with high school, they assured us. Apparently they looked at me and saw a potential cheerleading sorority girl in the raw, ready to be polished for action at any moment, unleashing those two years of private school and dance-class etiquette.

No matter how hard they tried to turn us into just-add-water Kennedys, all of this posturing failed, and so did college. The bottom line was that we were lower class, and there was no way we could be any different. As we were dragged nearly screaming off to college, the late-eighties economy steadily sank into the toilet. Their rental properties remained vacant, the beach house unrented; the cars wouldn't sell, and the real-estate market floundered. Their debt grew so out of control they were faced with declaring bankruptcy. All of the Realtors from the tropical vacation photos were declaring bankruptcy like dominoes, but my father couldn't deal with the shame. His suicide note was addressed mostly to his parents, and said how he had failed them by not being rich. He also declared his right, in the freest nation in the world, to choose death.

Our family was left in a sinkhole of debt. People came to the house during the funeral to claim cars and to try and buy the house. Everything was liquidated, and we all went our separate ways.

Despite my parents' arduous attempts at my reconstruction, I have retained bits of my native culture that will now be offered up to my daughter whether she likes it or not. Like eating green olives and watching *Lawrence Welk,* dirt-bike ganging and the art of survival in a classist nation, flamboyant American-flag apparel preferably worn in conjunction with a Mohawk or similar angst hairdo, and, most important, keeping a bag of bread on the table—not for fear of choking, or as a festering analogy to money, but to eat.

FILLING

Sailor Holladay

Why do my teeth hurt so badly? A deep, daily, thick, acute pain. It isn't just because I have nine cavities that need to be filled. I come from a long line of bad teeth. My granny had a full set of dentures before she turned thirteen. Her family was stationed in China at the time, during World War II. One of her teeth became infected and it spread through her whole mouth. She had every last one of her teeth pulled. My granny would tell us the love story about her meeting our gramps on the military base they lived on. He was a friend of her dad's and thought she was cute. One day he came up to her and introduced himself. She didn't say anything—she just flipped her top plate at him.

My teeth and I started out on better footing. I was my mom's last hope for oral glory. Topping her list of regrets were those braces she never had as a kid. She always said I had a chance in life, with my straight teeth. Unfortunately, when it came to predictions my mom's success rate was never very high: I got my first filling at age four. My kindergarten teacher sent me home with red pills I would scrub on my teeth, the dye sticking to the places I had plaque—red spots waving my toothbrush down, hoping to be seen, like road flares on a desolate highway. Those red pills never did much good—me and my little brother had contests to see who could go the longest without brushing. With no basic utilities or stable housing, dental hygiene wasn't a big priority.

We weren't always homeless, but if it wasn't the street it was a bus, a shack, or a trailer. Not a "look, Mommy, our house has wheels" kinda home, but a ten-foot-, maybe twenty-foot-long, "look, Mommy, the shower stall is above the toilet" kinda home. Being poor meant learning that Diehard is the best car battery to buy 'cause Sears'll let you recharge it for free, for life. Recharged batteries powered our television so we could watch *Full House* before doing homework by kerosene light. Being poor meant having lice until I was sixteen. Being poor meant going to twenty-five schools before graduating high school. Being poor meant having cold running water once in seven years. It meant putting used toilet paper in a bag next to the toilet because there wasn't a septic system, just a fifty-gallon barrel drum buried under the trailer, leaking sewage into the ground. Poor people don't conserve for political gain—there really ain't too much to waste. Once a week we'd haul ourselves down to the YMCA to shower. Mom would beg the attendant to waive the dollar charge until next time, or sneak us by. Other days we heated water on the stove and poured it into a basin. Dad washed first, Mom second, me third, and my two brothers last.

I've been plagued with nightmares ever since I can remember. They started when I was two years old. Often I dreamt my teeth were decaying and falling out. My handy dream dictionary states: "Dental problems, such as teeth falling out, being broken and so on, are the focus of many anxiety dreams, reflecting insecurities in the personal, domestic or professional sphere." Not only were my teeth dreams a reflection of waking-life anxieties and domestic troubles, they were a reflection of waking-life tooth trauma. It makes sense to me that my most compulsive ritual involves clicking my teeth. Ever since I can remember, I have been doing it: If I click my top and bottom teeth together on one side of my mouth, I have to click twice together on the other side and then click once more on the original side. I continue with this until I am satisfied that the pattern is symmetrical. This is one way that I release my anxiety through my teeth.

I remember one time when I was getting what was supposed to be a temporary crown put on after a root canal. I asked the dentist if I could get some kind of pain medication while I waited for another root canal months later. He sat me down and explained to me how "habit forming" painkillers can become. He lectured me against using any type of pain medication for fear that I would become addicted to it. I wondered then if having rotten teeth and no health insurance automatically serves as an identifier for drug addiction. If so, are both drug addicts and people with rotten teeth supposed to suffer in vain because we are told we brought it on ourselves? Preschools full of fluoride washes and flossing videos are insufficient when educating the poor—the "dentally challenged."

As the oldest kid in a poor family, I concerned myself with hustling ways to get milk on the table when the food stamps ran out. I concerned myself with whose stuff got pawned which month. Where I come from, if you have a mouth to feed, you've got two hands to work. Sometimes I wonder at how I knew so much about my family's financial matters. My middle-class friends who don't know how much money their parents make have always fascinated me; some don't even know what their parents do. When I first came into class consciousness at age sixteen, I called my mom to break the news: "Mom! We're working class!" She responded: "Oh, no, honey, we don't work." Her comment made me begin to understand the unique struggle all working people—but specifically poor people—face, fighting to survive in this society.

If people are ever confused about what class they belong to, housing, prior occupations, and access to education can all be good indicators as to where one might fit in. The condition of one's teeth is an even more accurate indicator. I would never tire of someone talking to me about their tooth trauma all day long, though most people don't want to have anything to do with such a conversation. Tooth problems are seen as a private matter, an ascribed condition.

Unlike some of my other poor friends, I did have the opportunity to visit the dentist a few times as a child. These visits began with excavating cavities and filling them with a metal amalgam that included mercury. Ten years later, mercury was reported to be potentially harmful, and when we got welfare insurance that covered dental procedures, my new dentist replaced all my old fillings with plastic composite ones. He even dug out and replaced all of Mom's old, dark-blue fillings. We were elated— no more metal coats of arms shining through our teeth, exposing them for the frail, chipping appendages they were. Three years later, when I was on my own at age sixteen, my beautiful white fillings started to leak. That shiny plastic became a symbol of what hid the reality of my life and class background: a pretty, quick fix for the much deeper underlying distress of poverty. Underneath their flawless exteriors were rotting teeth screaming to be drilled. Four root canals and one pulled tooth later, I was screaming, too.

I have always had a sorrowful relationship with my teeth—one filled with regret. If you have ever had a tooth pulled, maybe you understand. It was a sad, sad day when I had my first tooth extracted. It was pulled because I couldn't afford the eight hundred dollars cash it was going to cost me to get a root canal. The tooth had already been partially drilled by another dentist. As a tattoo artist often won't work on a tattoo by another artist, getting a dentist to finish another's drilling comes at a price. The music blared into my Walkman as I distracted myself from the dentist's chore. He put my tired tooth to sleep like a family dog that must be put down. Wrapping sophisticated pliers around my tooth, he rocked it back and forth, coaxing it out of my gums. I moaned in agony. My gums contracted and finally birthed their obstinate tooth. The vacancy that remains can never be filled.

REVERSE

Silas Howard

Donut Shoppe, 1978

I watch through the rain-streaked windows of the camper.

The Formica counters in the doughnut shop are chrome-lined, chipped, and faded to the color of Miami pools. Fluorescent lights flicker as the television plays: a blue Cycloptic giant announcing the news of the day: Christopher Reeve plays Superman, Carter meets with Middle East leaders at Camp David, and Jim Jones kills a congressman and then orders his followers to commit suicide. Sun-washed posters along the walls feature colossal close-ups of French crullers, maple doughnuts, and old-fashioneds. A couple sits drinking free refills and contemplating the responsibility of leaving town with a child, a fat golden retriever, seventy-five dollars in their pockets, and the camper. This is their escape hatch—a family vacation, an extended Sunday drive, travel through the nice neighborhoods to envision life in the ornate homes of the well-to-do.

At the doughnut shop that night they decided that, yes, they would go across the country. They would ignore the grinding, almost suffocating lack of money that kept them in a never-ending state of panic, a feeling that staying at home averred. This trip would be a clean slate, a new page, everything still to come. Necessity makes reality real.

I watched the highway from the bed that sat over the cab of the truck. Yellow lines moved hypnotically, miles and minutes passing, boredom into daydream. I wondered, my eyes wide as marigolds, where the dashes of yellow would take us. Like most kids I had ideas of what I wanted to be when I grew up, and many were the usual—veterinarian, farmer, Olympic figure skater. But when things were very chaotic, my ultimate fantasy was to grow up to be a housewife who watched TV, baked, and stayed home a lot. Things must have been bad during this time, 'cause I never remember having the dream so powerfully.

In the end I became allergic to security, as if it might pull me into a slumber and I'd wake up making donuts.

It never occurred to me that taking a family vacation on seventy-five dollars that lasted almost a year was strange until I talked about it with some friends recently. What, not all families take vacations this way? The "vacation" was scintillating and nerve-wracking. When there was no food, we always had television. Commercials filled with sexy, slow-motion shots of cheesy pasta dishes and tender prime rib steak.

The money lasted from Burlington, Vermont, all the way to that town in Virginia where some pilgrims landed, I forget the name. There we landed, tired, lost, and out of money. My stepmother got work as a cocktail waitress, and my father took a job at the local Red Lobster. The plan? Zoom to California and then drive back home again by the end of that summer. We made it to Atlanta, Georgia, my parents taking work along the way. The trip was extended past Christmas. Our family vacation lasted eight months and caused me to miss most of fifth grade.

By the end of that family vacation, the thing I wanted to be was an actor, California my mythical oasis. It was my obdurate belief that I need only set foot in Los Angeles and all my dreams would materialize. I wanted to be part of the lust-and-danger-drenched Hollywood fantasies that served as our weekend drug. Only I wanted to play the leading man—a role young girls were not encouraged to play.

Hollywood Forever

I now live in Hollywood and, while I'm not an actor, I did act in a movie my friend and I made titled *By Hook or By Crook*, a feature film that ended up winning several awards and being selected for Sundance. When Harry Dodge, my oldest friend and cowriter/director, and I were writing the script, we funded ourselves by hauling garbage. Two small, earnest guys filled with an ambiguous hope, to save people from the clutter of their material goods. There's big money in trash. Our only setback—we couldn't really afford the dump fees. Late at night we circumnavigated the industrial part of town looking for places to "store" our trash. Disposal turned out to be the hardest part of making money. All that effort to save fifty dollars. The risk of police and junkyard dogs. We'd tell people, "I didn't go to college, I went to haulage."

Nowadays I edit the added features that go on DVDs. Mainly I work on horror movies, where the bad girls get killed first and the college students are chased by—as one director put it—"cross-dressing retarded hillbillies." That's me, I think, though most people I know would protest. I need a T-shirt that reads, "No one knows I'm a cross-dressing, retarded hillbilly." The director states that his horror movie is about the generation gap—the youth running from the older, rural folks—but I think it's poverty they're running from. And run they should.

Everything is up for grabs in L.A., even the ground. Los Angeles is a horizontal city on shaky little legs. It is a city with no center, where things are hidden—especially true feelings. A place, they say, where you could die of enthusiasm. I love that about this town. My life as a myth. When trying to have more in your future than you did in your past, a vivid imagination is key. Fake it till you make it. The pathos of endless hope and possibilities, of being taken advantage of, *ahhh.* I could be discovered, maybe, just maybe . . . Yes, I realize "maybe" is a thin thread to hang one's hopes on, but I can still live next to my dreams and visit them—a little like having stuff in public storage.

Every day I wave at the sandwich man on my corner.

I drive by him every day. He stands on the corner with a handmade sign advertising inexpensive lunch specials. I think about his health and the tedium of it all. I think about him when I wonder what my next job will be now that I've moved from San Francisco to L.A. Actually, I don't imagine his face when I think of him, but rather the face of his costume, which is a large (from above his knees to a few feet above his head), sun-bleached sandwich with a shop logo on it. The sandwich is made of bread and floppy lettuce, and on the bread is a big smiling face with two huge eyeholes cut out of it, for the sandwich man to breathe through. His hands are big and padded like Mickey Mouse's, which I guess are the hands that a sandwich would have if a sandwich had hands. I wave to him when I'm stuck at that corner of Highland and Santa Monica.

When the sandwich guy waves back, he seems so enthusiastic that it breaks my heart, although perhaps it's only the big, cartoonish hands that I read as excited. It's quite likely that the guy wishes I'd stop waving at him like some five-year-old at the poor kids' Disney. Probably he should con-serve his energy. It can't be good for you, wearing a polyester suit in the middle of Los Angeles in summer, where the temperature frequently rises to 100 degrees. This is a dangerous combination—polyester, holding and shaking a sign, and the desert sun.

I had a friend who worked for an ice-cream shop as a bear one summer, and she had a whole padding of ice that she kept in the freezer to put on for work. "You can faint like *that*," she said, snapping her fingers for emphasis. Another friend of mine appeared on a talk show in an E.T. outfit. He nearly faded away because the costume was basically one of those rubber Halloween masks that almost killed you as a kid, but that went over your whole body. He was hunched over in the thing for an hour, waiting for his turn on the show, and by the time he got up there he was more like a sad, creepy, abused E.T. than the happy, bicycling-over-the-moon one from childhood. He made it offstage before passing out, but ended up, I imagine, depressing most of the audience.

Sometimes I see the sandwich walking home down Santa Monica Boulevard with his big square head slumped down. Of course, the tilt of his head may be a logistical thing—so he can see—but I choose to read it as a guy down on his luck stuck in this dead-end job as a sandwich. I make another vow to bring him a cool beverage with lots of ice. I wonder what his pay might be.

Later

"It's called IWS."

"What?"

"IWS—Inherited Wealth Syndrome."

This young man at a house party is telling me about his job with the Rockefeller family and the counseling service provided for inheritors and their spouses. This service helps with the trauma of having more wealth than you can comprehend; the trauma of feeling unworthy, for instance, since you will never be as great as the first Rockefeller, who made all the money.

"They have parties after these seminars with the staffers."

Oh, the wealthy must envy the staffers—"You make a finite amount of money? That's so amazing. Tell me, how do you spend your paycheck?" my friend jokes.

How many people have this syndrome, I wonder? I guess if you're that rich, it takes only three or four people to make it a bona fide disease. Quality over quantity. It's all about reimbursement, and if it's in the DSM, then insurance has to cover the treatment.

A woman sitting across from me explains her recent money-raising idea. She posted an offer on Craig's List that essentially read, "I will call and insult anyone you want for twenty-five dollars." You could tell her a time to call your boss, landlord, or ex-whatever, and she would come up with an inventory of insults that cut to the bone. The response was colossal—but no one wanted to pay. One guy wanted a date and she wrote back, "Who exactly are you asking out on a date, asshole?" The listing said nothing about her gender or sexuality. I thought her response to him was a good calling card for her work, but he didn't end up hiring her.

In L.A. there's what you say you do, and then what you do. Kind of like the Catholic Church, there's the official and the unofficial word. Officially I'm a director/actor/producer/designer/fill in the blank, but unofficially I'm a waitress/stylist/wedding singer/sandwich guy/fill in the blank. I'm the kind of director who takes the budget shuttle, not the limo. You can only exaggerate so far. Eventually they see what you drive and it's all over.

Recently, I started teaching a friend of mine to drive at the Hollywood Forever Cemetery, where people drive—not much, but a *wee* bit—slower. We crept by the Cadillac-sized tombstones with famous faces etched into granite lined by remunerative palms. Flowers from strangers line the graves; there's no love like the love for a stranger. Eventually we reached the back end of the cemetery and found a more humble section, where the tombstones sit like crooked little dog teeth. "This must be where the B actors get buried," my friend said.

"Well," I responded, "I guess they made it in, huh?"

MY MEMORY
AND WITNESS

Lis Goldschmidt and Dean Spade

Dean—

Hey. How's things in NYC? Tired here. Just home from hanging out with everyone. Feeling really tired of the class stuff we were talking about the other day. Tired of people fronting like they're poor or grew up poor or whatever—like it's cool to be poor. You know the deal. They put it on like an accessory. You know? Just like co-opting any culture. Do you know what I mean? It's like people who wear "native garb" from wherever they're exoticizing at the moment—but the thing is, they take it off when it gets old to them.

I guess I'm just feeling pretty pissed. Like I can't take it off. Like it *is* old. It's always been old. And makes me feel old and fucking tired. And small.

I don't mean to rant.

The main reason I'm writing is 'cause you carry the facts and I feel like I need them. You know the details that I think can help me not feel erased by these kinds of nights. You know how much Mom made. You know the welfare info. It sounds dumb—I know what it was like, but I've spent my whole life pretending it was something else, my whole life trying to pass

as something else—and I need the numbers to feel justified or
some shit. I need those numbers to prove me wrong or call me
out or something. Does that sound weird? It's like I've even
convinced myself . . . also like I want some fact to separate me
from those people.

I mean I remember it. I remember what it was like. I
remember the shame and all that. I remember that greedy
excited fucked-up feeling I got when she'd bring home the groceries. I remember swallowing myself one zillion times. I
remember being an invisible eyesore. I remember knowing this
couldn't be right. When I think of it now I get that same empty,
gagging thing. I remember that heavy fucking cloud that hung
around our tiny house. That fog that made it so hard to
breathe. That stress that kept us all quiet and angry and sad.
Remember?

I'm scrambling to think of something good and light, but
it goes back as far as I can remember. It only got darker and
heavier.

The end was the worst, right? I guess for me it was the
worst because I felt like I was the mom when she was sick. You
know? Not that we didn't both have to pick up what she could-
n't carry anymore. But I remember doing the grocery shopping
by myself. You know, I think it's really only the last maybe five
years that I don't have some crazy fear while in line at the grocery store. I think this is actually the first time I've really
thought about it. There's the shame of shopping at the discount
store. Scared someone from school would see us or something—and scared that if anyone ever came to our house (not
that they ever did), they'd see the bags from there. (Not to mention just seeing the house!) But then there were all the times we
had to put stuff back—do you remember that? I cringe thinking about it now. It was terrible. Embarrassing. I remember
being scared to look at Mom in that moment. How she'd look
it all over and have to decide what to put back. How did she do

that? How can you decide what food your three kids *don't* need? Can you imagine how stressful that must have been for her? *Ugh.* It fucking makes me want to puke. Then there was the shame of using food stamps. It's funny how kids I know now use food stamps with so much pride.

Dean, this sucks. I hate thinking about this stuff. I'm trying to reclaim it or something but sometimes it just feels like Mom trained us so well that passing is easier and the shame is too thick. Sometimes I think I'd make the world's greatest spy because I can pretend so well. Time to sleep.

I hope you're well—

I'm glad we have each other in this.

xo, Lis

Dear Lis,

I took this letter with me to Montreal where I was showing the film Tara and I are making about trans people and bathrooms. While I was there, friends of friends had a "white trash"–themed barbecue. The people I was staying with called the hosts to voice our protest to this theme, and heard that others were also upset, so we went anyway, thinking people wouldn't participate in the theme and that the message had gotten across. Of course, we were too optimistic. Many people came fake-pregnant, with giant Budweiser cans, fake southern accents, and severe blue eye shadow. What to do? I thought about how "trashy" it is for poor people to have children, how differently poor people's substance abuse is surveyed and punished, how easily these white people employed a term that suggests that all nonwhite people are trash while only some white people require such labeling. I thought about the time you were invited to a white-trash event where people were encouraged to black out their teeth, and I thought of how Mom lived her whole life hiding that she had dentures—like everyone in her family—from a time when "dental care for the poor" was pulling out all their teeth in adolescence. When she died I learned she had hidden this from me (you too?) my whole life—sleeping in uncomfortable dentures all those nights during our thirteen years together when I was too scared to sleep alone—all to hide from even me her poverty and shame. (Meanwhile I dreamt of the braces the other kids at school could afford.) I thought of my own consciousness, starting in elementary school, of the need to separate myself from the term "white trash." Be careful how you smell, who sees your house. Try to get Mom not to curse or smoke in front of other people's parents.

But at this party I bit my tongue and turned my head when they arrived in costumes. Couldn't bring myself to speak on this rooftop full of people I had just met. I spend sixty to eighty hours a week exclusively talking about poverty and advocating for poor people, but I could not advocate for myself, could not give up the small amount of passing, of blending in. We left fast and Pascal, Brianna, and I ranted on the street, wondering how we should have handled it, talking about how girl–social conditioning still operates in our trans bodies, convincing us we shouldn't confront. With every passing hour I've become more irate. No place to put it. More anger to add to the churning crushing pile that lives behind my sternum.

Tired. I hear you about being tired. I'm tired of being diplomatic about poverty. Tired of trying to convince rich people at nonprofits, rich people at foundations, and rich gay people especially to care about and support the lives of low-income intersex and trans people. I'm tired of helping them notice that we exist, trying not to make them too uncomfortable to give money to the struggle that (when we win, which we will) will end wealth and poverty for everyone. Tired of being gentle and nonthreatening and helping them appease the guilt about their hoarding lifestyles so they can act a little. And I'm tired of hearing that you're getting paid less than the private-college educated man who sits next to you doing the same job, and tired of seeing all my trans friends without jobs or adequate housing and trapped in the criminal-injustice system. I'm tired of other poverty lawyers (from upper-class backgrounds) telling me I don't pay myself enough when I make twice what Mom supported four people on in the years she had jobs, and when our clients are fighting like hell for a couple hundred bucks a month from welfare or ten bucks to make a call from jail. I have to figure out how to not get too tired. Sometimes I think that's what killed our mom. Somehow, you and I got out of there, out of that dirty house, off those gravel roads, out of Virginia, but she didn't make it. I think all the time of what it would be like if she could see us now—if I could make her a fancy dinner in my apartment (artichokes) and take her to see something city-beautiful; if, for her birthday, we could fly her to San Francisco and all three of us could have tea in your kitchen and walk around Golden Gate Park and she'd tell us the names of all the flowers. It's almost Mother's Day.

You asked for the facts. I carry them around like the chip on my shoulder. The most she ever made was $18,000 one year. Our welfare was less than $400 a month. We got a total of $50 when we three spent Saturdays cleaning the glass and mirror store, less when we cleaned houses. The social security survivors benefits our foster parents got for us were about $500 a month each until we turned eighteen. (It's sick that she could support us better by dying but there was not money to help keep her alive.) The jacket she always wanted when she was in middle and high school, that all the other kids had but she never got, cost $7.02 Canadian. The most important fact, maybe, is that if we'd been in the same situation after the 1996 welfare cuts, we wouldn't have been entitled to the same benefits because of her immigration status, and, in my estimation, we would have had a much harder time keeping a place to live or staying together as a family as long as we did.

I love you, Lis. You're my memory and my witness, and my only connection to all that we've lost. I love that you keep the sweatpants Mom got in rehab and that I slept in when you were caring for me after my chest surgery. When I'm not biting my tongue, it's because I'm thinking of how quickly you call people on their shit, how vicious your wit can be, and how you always have my back.

Love, Dean

WINGS

tatiana de la tierra

Placing a pink-feather headband in my hand, my abuelita Blanca kissed me goodbye, crying. I cried, too. I didn't know why. The perpetually gray Bogotá skies joined in, sprinkling us with cold rain. I ran up the narrow metal staircase as wind bit my wet cheeks, into an airplane that would take me and my family far from Colombia. It was May 1968 and I had just turned seven years old.

Thick, warm Atlantic air greeted us as we clambered, wide-eyed, out of our metal cocoon. The air in Miami was nothing like the air I knew in the Andean mountains. But being yanked from the love and protection of my aunts, grandmothers, and great-aunts was the most momentous change. It was bigger than air itself. I walked to the market with them, chit-chatted on the sidewalk, made corn arepas at the crack of dawn, collected eggs in the morning, accompanied them in the evening for hot chocolate. They cooked for me, bought dresses for me, introduced me to all their friends. But in Miami, everybody was a stranger.

At the airport I played with stairs that moved and doors that opened magically. A strange twig of a man who wore ripped denim and spoke halting Spanish greeted us. "Yo aquí para ayudarte," he said, offering a warm handshake. Harvey was a friend of a friend of my dad's; they embraced as if they already knew each other. My mom looked at him cautiously through her reddened eyes. Finally, she extended her hand.

Everything seemed brand-new and shiny those first few days. All the blades of grass were uniformly green and stood properly on plush manicured lawns. The clean-shaven policemen wore immaculate starched uniforms and drove sleek cars crowned with little blue and red domes that sometimes flashed and made wailing noises. Neat rows of containers housing exotic foods filled the spotless stores, where clerks counted crisp bills over Formica counters and gave back the change without stealing. Exquisite paintings graced cereal boxes and cans of soup, and luminous rays emanated from curvy Coca-Cola bottles branded with fire-red labels.

My father took me to a 7-Eleven, where I marveled at the cans decorated with vivid color images of the foods they contained.

"This one, Papi," I said. We both scrutinized the can. It had a picture of reddish brown beans on the label. Beans, a mainstay of our diet, had to be soaked in water the night before and took hours to cook. Yet here they were in the palm of our hand, ready to eat. We went home with the can. My father opened it and heated up the beans with some rice. I could tell they were different; they were watery and didn't smell right. Still, I brought a spoonful to my mouth. I gagged as the flavor hit my palate. They were sweet. Beans were supposed to be salty and spiced with onions, garlic, tomato, and peppers. They were supposed to be thickened with green plantains. They were not supposed to be sweet or watery.

My mom, who disliked cooking and had little time for it, took advantage of the cheap and instant foods. She went grocery shopping and came home with Kool-Aid, white bread, processed cheese, frozen chicken potpies, sugar-coated cereals, and Hamburger Helper. The Colombian foods I was accustomed to—fresh blackberry juice, farmer's cheese, Creole potatoes, tamales, and empanadas—quickly became memories.

But my dad's hunger for familiar foods roared incessantly. He enjoyed eating and cooking, and he went to great lengths to find magical ingredients. He discovered that you could find fresh coconut milk in the shell, ripe guanabanas, cumin powder, and plantains in bodeguitas like La Ideal and Los Pinareños. You could get an entire meal—a bandeja paisa with real arepas—

at La Fonda, a Colombian restaurant. One day, my father took the bus and went foraging, his eyes bulging with visions of Colombian food. He returned late in the afternoon, his shirt splattered with drops of sancocho, his breath greasy from fried empanadas, his belly expanded with sobrebarriga, his fingers sticky with dulce de leche. He was beaming. He brought us avocados, coconuts, yucca, plantains, and Colombian delicacies.

On Saturdays we took the bus to Miami Beach and went swimming by the pier, on the southern tip. There, I dug my toes into the sand and bobbed in the salty ocean. My mom, who was pregnant, sat on the beach and read a book while the rest of us played in the water. We ate peanut-butter-and-jelly sandwiches and drank Kool-Aid. Once, as a treat, we went to Kentucky Fried Chicken after being at the beach all day. They had a special offer—two pieces of chicken with a biscuit and a small Styrofoam cup of mashed potatoes and gravy for $1.29. We got a special and sat down to share the food. I bit into a drumstick. It was good, crunchy and spicy. But as I swallowed I recalled what had happened the day before we left for Miami, and my stomach became queasy.

We were in El Libano, at my great-aunt's house. It was our last day there. I was in the corridor that faced the garden when I saw that Cuki, my favorite chicken, was being hunted down. "Run, Cuki, run!" I screamed as I saw a shiny machete swinging in her direction. I gripped the wooden porch railing as she ran, headless, fluttering her golden brown wings in a futile attempt to levitate. Cuki, who used to peck at my feet when I showered on the patio beneath blue skies, was our last supper. I missed her, and I missed the black earth that caked my feet when I played in my great-aunt's garden.

Our first home in our new world was a room in Harvey's house. Blond, blue-eyed, and eccentric, Harvey slept on the beach, washed dishes for a living, and drank rainwater that he collected in an oxidized metal container in the back yard. He nourished himself on tropical concoctions, blending whole papayas with fish guts and honey. Restaurant napkins for toilet paper and roadside-discarded produce for dinner were his gifts. He taught my mom to walk on the grass to extend the life of shoe soles. He came home every few days to drink the rainwater, wash up, and change clothes. Harvey didn't believe in pesticides so roaches crawled freely on the walls—and on us. He didn't believe in banks or the government, either. His living-room library was stocked with books about politics, anthropology, and history. He let us live in his house for free, until we could afford to rent a place on our own.

Another Colombian family soon joined us, moving into the room across the hall. The coziness of our home disappeared with the violent intrusion of our new neighbors. José Miguel was my dad's military companion from Colombia. He was a construction worker, thick and muscular, who wore a constant snarl on his face and stank of liquor. His wife, Irma, took care of us while my parents worked. One day, my mom came home earlier than expected. My brother and sister and I were cowering in our room as José Miguel beat Irma. Their little girls, Nubia and Cacallo, were screaming throughout the house. My mom grabbed a broomstick and busted in on him. "Béstia!" she yelled, leading a sobbing Irma into our room.

The scenes repeated like tired reruns. When José Miguel wasn't home we were free to run and play, but as soon as we heard his boots step into the house, we froze. "¡Chito!" we warned each other, walking on tiptoes, trying to be invisible.

But not everything was bad, because I was with my brother, Gustavo Alberto, and my sister, Claudia. They were my only friends. The three of us walked around the neighborhood together, marveling at the gringo houses and the gringo lawns and the gringo postman and the gringo talk. Gone were the mountains that ringed Bogotá, the matriarchs in the countryside, the gamines who begged for money on the street, the fresh air. We didn't understand why we had left Colombia or what the future held for us. So we did what we knew how to do, no matter where we were. We played. We ran and kicked bottles, climbed trees, played tag. We dueled as cowboys and Indians. I wore my pink-feather headband and protected my tribe. My brother brandished his miniature machete. My sister was the village elder, scheming to outwit the troops.

In August, three months after our arrival, my little sister was born. Natasha came home in a white wicker crib that my mom had bought used for $1.50. Cushioned with a new white satin pad and lined with blankets, pink balloons floating on the flannel, the crib wobbled on uneven legs. Natasha, who was conceived in Colombia, was the only U.S. citizen in my family. She was a real gringa and even had golden hair. She was my life-size doll. I changed her diapers, prepared her bottles, and cradled her in my arms.

My childhood had come to a close. Summer was ending and school was about to start. Irma found a job and couldn't take care of us anymore. My mom worked as a maid in the Tudor Hotel in Miami Beach and my dad worked in a paper factory. I was the oldest, so my responsibilities increased. I began to cook, clean, and take care of my siblings. I became a miniature adult. "Wash that plate!" I scolded. "Clean up that mess!" I nagged. But I never got the response to my commands that I expected.

If we hadn't left Bogotá I would still have been wearing my gray uniform to school and learning to pray the rosary. I would have come home to my mom and played outside and done my homework and had arroz con lentejas for dinner. I would have been a seven-year-old girl just like all the others. But Bogotá grew more distant every day. After four months in Miami it seemed that we were there for good.

School was an enclosed city surrounded by banyan trees and hibiscus bushes where I became indoctrinated into another culture. Gimnasio Palestina, my first grade school in Bogotá, was a private school in a small brick building. But Shadow Lawn Elementary took up an entire block. It was made of concrete and had dozens of classrooms, a cafeteria, a gymnasium, and a playground. In Bogotá my school had one class and one teacher, but in Miami there were hundreds of students, many teachers, and a principal. I was the only light-skinned girl in my class and one of the few Spanish-speakers in the entire school. I couldn't speak English and was just beginning to understand some of the words.

I sat in silence at my desk with a thick pad of baby-blue-lined paper and a yellow No. 2 pencil that had been given to me for free on the first day of school. Mrs. Clara sent students to the chalkboard to write words that she dictated. She called on me; I stood at the front, looking at my feet, frozen. She read her list: ocean, river, stream. I fingered the chalk and she repeated the words, eventually chanting them as if they were commands. "Ocean! River! Stream!" I didn't even attempt to write on the board; I went back to my desk, my fingertips dusted with white chalk.

I dreaded those public moments that highlighted the fact that I was a foreigner. Sometimes I sat at my desk plotting my revenge. I would master the English language. I would infiltrate the gringo culture without letting on that I was a traitor. I would battle in their tongue and make them stumble. I would cut out their souls and leave them on the shore to be pecked on by vultures.

One pivotal afternoon, I squirmed in my seat. I had an itch between my legs like a red-hot ant bite. Finally, I reached my hand toward the ceiling to ask for permission to go to the bathroom. Mrs. Clara looked at me; I knew no words to express my state of emergency. I pointed to the door; she stared back blankly. The whole class looked on. I grabbed my crotch, squeezed and grimaced. Finally, she understood, but as I darted out of the room, warm pee exploded between my legs, trickling into my socks and splashing in droplets on the floor. I ran out of school, my moist shoes pounding on the speckled tile, squeaky drumbeats echoing in the corridor.

Past the banyan tree by the playground and through the neighboring streets, I sprinted as if I were being pursued. I ran with the insides of my legs soiled, wet, and sticky with urine, sucking oxygen into my bursting lungs with wrenching gulps. I wished that the stiff metal airplane that had ripped me from my home would take me back. Pumping my arms, I wished for silver angel wings that glided or long, broad eagle wings that soared. But I knew that my flapping was useless.

THERE ARE HOLES IN MY MANDARIN DOG BISCUIT

Shell Feijo

The stretch of my favorite shirt as I pulled it over my still-damp hair helped ease me into the day ahead. Going to school had never been easy and middle school at MLK had proved to be no exception. The teasing had begun almost as soon as I climbed onto the bus for the first time. Words like "greasy," "dirty," "smelly," "pizza face," "poor," "trash," "welfare case," and so on engulfed me on a daily basis. But, I had found friends and muddled through, making jokes at my own expense until the teasing subsided. After all, the rest of the kids on the bus weren't much different. They were probably just using me to get the focus off of their own clothes, smells, lives.

Anyway, I smiled that morning getting dressed—I always felt good when the red-and-white-striped T-shirt that I loved fell snug against my chest. As I turned to leave, my mother reached out and grabbed my shoulder, saying, "You aren't wearing that, there's a hole in it."

I pulled away. "Everything I have has something wrong with it. This is my favorite."

"I don't give a shit. You are *not* wearing a shirt with a hole in it."

I started to cry. I ran back to my room, grabbed a dirty sweatshirt, and yanked it on, tears streaking down my face. I ran down the six flights of stairs and out into the sweet stench of a Berkeley morning, hoping I wouldn't miss the bus and have to walk.

I thought about the hole in the shirt a lot that day, as though I were wishing the shirt back into its pre-hole existence, the worn-in comfort that it had had the day we bought it at the thrift store. I felt empty without the T-shirt holding me tight, cold without its striped warmth. When I wore it I imagined there was no pain, no queasiness, no hunger. But soon the shirt was forgotten; more pressing issues were at hand.

Rushing home after school, my stomach would groan and shift, crying out with after-school hunger pangs and butterflies of hope that my mother would not be home when I got there. I climbed the stairs, silently praying that when I rounded the dark hallway I would see the outline of a note, taped glistening to the door. When it was there, it meant going in and sighing with relief, making a baked potato when we had a bag, or getting a cup of the sugarless cheap drink that nobody else's mom made them drink. My mom had to be the hippie welfare mom, no Kool-Aid or Skippy peanut butter here. Only chunks of natural peanuts in a layer of oil, and pure, juice-flavored water. Some days, I would rush home and in note-inspired bliss I would wander the apartment, imagining that my mom would never come home, never yell again, never hit, never cry, never stare at me with the hurt of her whole life transferring to me, through me. Other days, the hunger would be too much, and I would search the kitchen, thinking maybe I had missed some small piece of cheese, or a leftover piece of chicken in the fridge. Never had anything been overlooked, but there was always the box on top of the fridge.

It never failed that no matter how poor we were, how much we struggled to stretch the food stamps or the social-security check my mom got for being legally blind, mentally ill, and unemployed, the dog, the beautiful Doberman my mom had gotten for protection, always had bones. Purina dog biscuits, at that.

The first time, I tried them at my mother's demand. She said there was nothing for dinner that night, and that dog biscuits were really made out of "people food."

"Really," she said, "they have more nutrients than anything I would cook. If you are that hungry, eat one." Dog biscuits taste like crunchy box. No flavor, just crunch, and a mealiness that makes you feel full even when you have tasted nothing of any substance. I guess they must taste different to dogs. But, they weren't so bad. They weren't like rancid meat or anything, more like a really healthy granola bar from the overpriced natural food co-op around the corner.

The taste of the dog biscuits was better than the acid pinch of memory that comes to me as a mandarin orange. Mandarin oranges and I go way back. Back to the couple of months we lived in Albany, in the rented house with the fat tree in the yard. The house with roaches crawling under the kitchen sink and over the walls when the dark descended at night. The house where the electricity got shut off. The house where my mom and her latest boyfriend smoked and snorted, stayed in bed all day and yelled all night. The house where a sleepover turned into torture, all on account of those damn mandarin oranges.

My best friend, Nikki, had come on the BART train alone, all the way from Concord. We had overnight plans of giggling and reading together, snacking and sipping ice-cold Coke late into the night, covering up the glare of low-battery-flickering flashlights with torn blankets and just the right angle of bodily shield. Nikki was the only friend I would ever invite over, the only one who could be trusted with my secrets, the only one I had ever known with secrets of her own. The night of the mandarin oranges is the last night I remember us together. Maybe she was scared to come back. Maybe my secrets had proved to be too deep.

We were hungry and there was nothing to eat. I don't mean that there was only peanut butter and jelly, or milk instead of juice; I don't mean that there was nothing we liked. I mean there was nothing there. I walked down the hall apprehensively, the familiar butterflies grinding against my stomach, and knocked quietly on my mom's bedroom door. She answered in her nightgown. I told her we were hungry and asked if she had any money for us to go to the store.

Clutching the five-dollar bill with delight, I chased after Nikki, screaming that I would catch her as we approached the nearby Lucky's. We slowed to a fast walk, sweat pooling with kid-funk on us as we laughed and entered the shiny mecca of food. We struggled past the potato-chip aisle and stole peeks at the bakery cookies. We had my mom's last five, and a TV dinner apiece was what we were allowed to get. I chose the veal parmigiana, a 99-cent favorite, and Nikki picked the Salisbury steak meal. We held hands and waited to check out in the express lane.

I know I had the five. I had been holding it so tight I could still feel its crinkle, its damp presence in my palm. The checker glared at me and said, "Do you have the money or not?" I started to panic and could feel tears welling up. Nikki tried to help, and took off through the store's aisles, scanning for the wrinkled bill. After an eternity standing there and the realization that the money was gone, I asked the checker to hold the dinners while we searched on the street. We walked back and forth in a crisscross pattern, without saying a word. I was supposed to bring back the change—the three dollars left over—and dinner for Nikki and me.

Finally, we gave up. It was very dark and my tears had turned to sobbing. Nikki let me lean on her and we slowly edged home, so different from the girls who had bounded toward the store. I turned the knob slowly and tried to sneak in. My mom was waiting. She was mad. "Where have you been? It's been over an hour."

I started to tell her that I was sorry. I wanted her to know that I really didn't mean to lose the money. I said, "Mom, I don't know what happened. I was holding the money real tight but when I went to pay, it was gone." *Whack!* She slapped me hard, and turned to Nikki. "What did you two buy?"

"Nothing," Nikki said. "We picked frozen dinners and then the money was gone." My mom took my arm and dragged me into the kitchen. "Well," she said, "now you are going to eat what I fix. The last of my cigarette money." She mumbled for a while, slamming empty cabinets and cursing. Nikki stood transfixed, wedged into the corner of the kitchen, staring at my mom.

"Come here," my mom said. "Get in line."

Nikki stood behind me and my mom opened a large can, placing it in front of me with one fork. "Take turns eating one bite at a time, and finish the whole thing. This is your dinner." I tried to swallow, but the tanginess stung my tongue and the crying had made my throat tighten. I didn't even feel hungry anymore. I started to spit and my mom yelled, "Oh, no, you wanted dinner, you lost the last of my money, you are going to eat." Nikki stepped in front of me and grabbed the fork, taking a huge bite. The liquid sprayed, making my face sticky, and Nikki reached for another section of orange. I think she was trying to save me from eating it. My mom pushed her out of the way and told me to eat up.

I tried again, and this time the force of the fork plunged against my gag reflex, and I threw up everywhere. My mom paused. For a moment, I thought she was going to make me eat it. Instead, she said, "You girls have had dinner. Now clean this shit up and get to bed."

We cleaned late into the night and fell asleep from sheer exhaustion. We never did play that night, tell stories, or giggle. We fell asleep listening to the sounds of each other's growling bellies, and woke to my mom thanking her boyfriend for a bag of food. We ate cereal that morning, and cold milk. No one ever mentioned the canned mandarin oranges.

Locked in my mind is a mist of childhood experiences like this one. They run together—food, clothes, pets, houses, fights, family—intertwined with each other, flowing and stopping as they wish, resisting separation into neat categories. These childhood experiences all revolve around money, and the lack thereof. As I reflect on them now, twenty years later, they boil down to one memory, an amalgam that reminds me, that speaks to me, that scares me: There are holes in my mandarin dog biscuit.

MY SEASON OF
PAPER DRESSES

Colleen McKee

At the South County, Missouri, Department of Health clinic (affection-
ately known as the DOH), surrounded by that je ne sais quoi ambiance
particular to government offices, I squirmed in my hot plastic chair, trying
not to look at the clock. I also tried not to look at the chairs, which, unfortunately, were puce-colored. The walls, of course, were green, like lima
beans. I thought, They paid someone to decorate this room, they paid
someone with my tax money to decorate this room, someone who probably has health insurance. But O.K., these people are here to help me, and
everyone knows what beggars can't be, so . . . I tried not to think about
that, either.

Even though I was mercifully free of female trouble (unless you
counted my ex, Antoinette), I was waiting to put my ankles in the stirrups
for a Pap smear. Why? Because of DOH policy. Before one could be examined for one's complaint—in my case, a productive cough (now, doesn't
that sound nice, "a productive cough," as though my cough was really
working hard for me?), one first had to have a blood test, an HIV test, and,
in the event of femaleness, a Pap smear. Only then could one make an
appointment to be examined for what actually ailed one. When I first
called the clinic, in May 1995, I had already had the cough for three
months. It typically took three weeks to a month to get an appointment,

and you had to have an appointment for every Pap smear and test. In my
case, this included two appointments the DOH had canceled. They had
not, however, found it necessary to notify me of said cancellations, as this
was not their policy.

Finally, an orderly called my name from behind his cubicle of bullet-
proof glass, and I was led to a tiny olive-drab room with a rickety table. I
changed into a lovely paper dress in which I resembled a paper-towel roll
and filled out a long questionnaire. Then I sat there for an hour, check-
ing out the syringes and reading interesting brochures on sexually
transmitted diseases. A very tired-looking blond woman finally entered
the room and said, "Hi, I'm Dr. So-and-So." She looked over the questionnaire and asked me a few questions, which, incidentally, were already
on the questionnaire.

"Age?"

"Twenty-one."

"Are you sexually active?"

"Well . . ." I wasn't sure how to answer. Antoinette had just walked out on
me two weeks before, leaving me with nothing but a long summer of doctor's
appointments and brooding over endless cups of tea with gay men.

"Let's put it this way," said the doctor. "When was the last time you had
sex?"

"Two weeks ago."

"A man or a woman?"

Great, I thought, she's not going to assume I'm straight. She's going to
be cool about this.

"A woman."

"Did you use a condom?" the doctor asked me.

"I beg your pardon?"

"Did you use a condom?"

"No, ma'am, I had sex with a woman."

"Are you taking birth control pills?"

"No, ma'am, I had sex with a woman."

"Are you trying to get pregnant?" she asked, exasperated.

I wasn't really sure how to tell this doctor that there was no chance that

Antoinette could have impregnated me. I considered drawing her a diagram, since I had all that paper in the form of my dress. Instead, I said, "No, ma'am, I had sex with a woman. I have not had sex with a man in a year. When I had sex with a man, we used condoms."

She stared at me as though I had just announced I had sodomized the Pope.

"Do you mean to tell me," she said, "you had sex with a man and a woman at the same time?"

"No, ma'am. Two weeks ago, I had sex with a woman. One woman, and myself, alone."

The room was dead silent as she continued to stare at me in undisguised horror. In my paper dress on the cold steel table, I felt like some strange specimen at the zoo, one that wasn't supposed to exist. And I wish I could tell you I said something really funny to her. But we both just sat there and stared, I in my paper dress and she in her doctor's cloak. Until finally she sighed and said, "I'll need you to put your feet in the stirrups, please, and then I'll need to do an anal probe." And I just stared at the ceiling, trying not to think about that either.

At last the blood test, HIV test, and Pap smear were over, and it was time to have that cough examined. So on a relentlessly bright August day, my mom grimly schlepped me back to the clinic in her 1973 Buick. "I sure hope they find something out," Mom said. "You know what I been thinking, though?" There was that note of angry suspicion in her voice that always makes my stomach clench.

"What?"

"Well, I've just been thinking about all them years we spent in Times Beach."

"Yeah?" Times Beach, Missouri, is a little town—well, not so much a town as a sprawl of trailers bordered by the Meramec River, a horse pasture, and a highway—well known in Missouri as the first town in the nation to have been completely evacuated due to toxic waste. This was just one more thing I did not want to think about.

"Well, me and your dad moved out there when you were three, and I was pregnant with Alexis . . . so that was '77. We lived there three years. Now, they laid that dioxin down in '72, but see, no one on the beach knew that. We thought it was just regular oil they sprayed, to keep the dust down."

"Yeah, but it didn't even do that, did it? I remember it was really dusty there."

Mom snorted. "No, it didn't keep no dust down. Dust got all over everything, you couldn't even keep your house clean out there."

"Right," I said. "Because I remember playing in the dust outside the trailer. I liked to scoop it into my Tonka dump truck."

"Yeah, you did. I couldn't stop you. You were like Pigpen from *Peanuts*, always surrounded by a cloud of dust."

I almost laughed at that, but found that I just couldn't. I was thinking about something. There was a tightness in my chest. "Wait," I said. "But what I don't understand is this: They sprayed in '72, so didn't people start getting sick by the time we moved there?"

"Sure they did, lots of people were sick, and the animals were too. I tell you, when I lived there I would wheeze and cough, sometimes until I passed out. And the whole reason your dad and I lived there in the first place is because we thought the country was a healthy place to raise kids!"

"Then why didn't they evacuate it until '82?"

"Well, my neighbors told me they tried to get the EPA and the DOH out there almost ten years before that, when the horses started dying, but they never even showed up. It was just poor people, you know? It was all poor people living out there."

She patted my hand. Her hand was cold. "I don't mean to scare ya, babe. I wish I had the money to take you to a nice doctor's office, but I just don't have it."

"Oh, Mom, that's O.K. You don't have to apologize."

"But," she said, a little too cheerfully, "I did bring you some *Incredible Hulk* comics to look at."

"All right, Mom!"

Inside, Mom and I parked it on those puce chairs and tried to forget about dioxin, the Department of Health, and everything else. She told me about her most recent painting, "The Incredible Hulk vs. the Grateful Dead." I have always wished I could turn myself into the Incredible Hulk.

I think that then I would not spend so much time in waiting rooms. As it was, I waited for two and a half hours that day before I was led to the examining room. Then I waited another hour and a half to see the doctor, this time a Chinese woman named Lorraine, who giggled, "Oh, I didn't know you were in here."

Dr. Lorraine decided I had a cold.

"In August? A cold? For five months?"

"That's right. I give you some Robitussin." (Which the clinic generously supplied.)

After two weeks of slurping Robitussin with no results, I made another appointment, and four weeks later I was back, this time for a diagnosis of the flu (in September? for six months?), for which I was prescribed a course of antibiotics—and a different kind of Robitussin.

I was not surprised to find myself at the clinic again six weeks later, this time for a tuberculosis test—which was negative, thank god, since if I did have tuberculosis, by that time I would have been dead. And six weeks after that, I was told to schlep up to the Berkeley Department of Health clinic for lung X-rays.

And one month later, at long last, I had a firm diagnosis:

"There is nothing wrong with you," said Dr. Lorraine. "You just like to cough."

"I assure you, ma'am, I do not like to cough."

"No," she said, laughing merrily. "You just like to cough."

"No, no no no no. I do not enjoy coughing."

"Here. I give you some Robitussin."

"Ma'am, I already have some Robitussin. I have three bottles of Robitussin. I have Robitussin Expectorant, I have Robitussin PM, I even have Robitussin Extra Strength!"

"Bye-bye. You go home and rest now."

Four years later I found myself in another clinic's emergency room, this time for undiagnosed asthma and a major infection of my skin, sinuses, lungs, vagina, and ears. All at the same time. I was red and white and blue all over, like some kind of patriotic joke. As I had told you-just-like-to-cough Lorraine, I spent my formative years in dioxin-soaked

Times Beach, for which no one has ever taken responsibility—not the Environmental Protection Agency, who ignored the problem for nearly ten years; not the St. Louis Department of Health, who didn't want to get their hands dirty; certainly not Monsanto, who created the napalm by-product in the first place. And why should they take responsibility? What kind of trailer-trash fools lived there anyway? Hell, if the dioxin hadn't given so many of us infected lungs and cancer, we'd probably just have frittered our days away smoking and drinking, eating cheesy puffs and Ho-Ho's, screwing our relatives and giving each other AIDS. At least all that time spent standing in line for food stamps and doctors kept us out of trouble.

So what's the moral of the story, if you're poor and from Missouri? Take two of these, drink two tablespoons of that, don't ask questions, don't screw around, and whatever you do, please don't call us in the morning.

WHAT I ATE WHERE

Diane di Prima

summer 1953—lamb chops, fresh tomatoes, and pepperidge farm bread. this was the time of the chic girl and sometimes she came to visit and stayed to supper and she would eat nothing but lambchops or steak and sometimes a boiled vegetable with a little butter and pepperidge farm whole wheat bread with butter on it. which got to be very boring and i ate a lot more of it than she did because i never knew when she would come to dinner. she used my pad during the day when i was at work and i still remember how it was one day to come home and find her asleep in her slip, the white of the slip, the white of the sheets, and her skin, flushed with the afternoon sun on it.

fall 1953—kraft cheese spreads on pepperidge farm bread for lunch, this at work while doing latin, i was reading vergil i think, i worked in the credit department of a large sugar company.

february 1954—lunch tongues, liver spread, caviar, vienna sausages, anything that came in small enough jars. we lived off what we could steal from the a&p, sue had a navy coat with big stiff sleeves, i had a trenchcoat with nice deep pockets, and jeri would slip a steak under his jacket cross his arms over his breast and swish out, rolling his eyes at the boys at the counter. we always bought bread.

spring 1955—a lot of scrambled eggs, at other people's pads. lived nowhere, had keys to a lot of places, and it seems whatever people are out of they always have a couple of eggs left. hate eggs.

summer 1955—potato pancakes in the back of a bookstore where i worked. the only store open by the time i remembered to shop being always a delicatessen with frozen potato pancakes, we thrived on potato pancakes, sour cream, and coffee. night after night. me, and tim who was my lover, and ed who was blond and silent and who i have never yet seen enough of.

winter 1955–56—english muffins four am at rudley's because no one could sleep, susan's lover, an actor, having a peculiar propensity for brooding, or talking on the phone, or getting into the wrong bed in this case my bed, in the middle of the night and creating general insomnia. after enough shifts and turns and muffled sighs one of us would finally sit bolt upright and say Let's go out for coffee, and that would finish the night. rudley's was on central park and the dawns were nice.

fall 1956—hopping john, which is brown rice and beans and wine and ham hocks; or else lentils and chicken gizzards with wine; or garbage soup which was everything cheap thrown into the pot. cooked in a four-gallon kettle, enough for everybody, payment was always you brought up some wood for the fireplace. food was warm all night, you just took a bowl and sat down. nobody ever talked much, we looked at the fire.

is there a meal i remember, i mean a real meal? do i remember a meal? i remember my first chicken in white wine in a restaurant and my first lobster but they were not meals to remember. what i do remember are snacks again, more snacks.

i remember onion soup at rumpelmayer's very late it must have been. one of those nights it was that one doesn't like to remember it is still happening somewhere in space and time somewhere in the navel of one's horror and not a night to remember lightly but i remember it. or rather it still is here, to be talked about. its tail is curled, i swear, around its feet.

we had gone to dinner yes in the gold coin, whatever it's called, something like that in the chic east fifties with an Old Family Friend. it was chinese food but so expensive you didn't know it was chinese, i mean there were no fried noodles or wonton soup, just all these strange things, and very good. then the Old Family Friend and i had an argument, which i will not mention by name, as it is sitting right here staring at me and it is bad manners to talk about a thing to its face. a very bad argument. purple feet, its tail is curled around, you can see for yourself. anyway it was the kind that ends with you are killing your parents, what right have you got to breathe out just because you breathed in, and there are already too many babies in new york.

so i got up and left the gold coin and it was raining and the men at the door said what was wrong with the service and should they call a cab and i said no, nothing and no, i had of course no money for a cab. so i walked to 60th street in the rain and waited for a crosstown bus, and home, where i vomited for the first time in my life from anger and cried for the millionth time in my life from anger i scarcely ever cry from anything else. vomited i remember right on the floor, sitting on the bed and crying, vomited. which splashed my new shoes or were they sneakers, i can't remember now but they were new at the time and it never quite came off; and splashed all over this orange face of a woman that pete had painted on the floor and we used to call it the face on the barroom floor though it wasn't like that at all, very stylized and still. there had been no more walls to paint on so he had painted on the floor.

and i got up and cleaned up the mess with some old clothes which i decided then and there were rags and threw water on it and put newspaper on the water and sat down again on the edge of the bed and looked at the newspapers and i think i probably started to cry again. and in came susan who had been dining with us and though she more or less agreed with me would never have left such a good meal to gesturize, i mean walk out with me, only she came by after to see how i was and she saw. so she said, get dressed again, and wash your face, and let's go out and do something festive, and she was right. she was almost always right about festivities, it was just the times in between that she was wrong in and they were most of the time.

so i knew she was right this time and i got dressed again and we went to rumpelmayer's, which was one of the few places open at that hour. we could now that i think of it have gone to the russian tearoom, but maybe we didn't have enough money, i don't know, i know i didn't and you can always get a snack at rumpelmayer's. what i mean to say is rumpelmayer's is sue's idea of someplace festive but not mine at all, it's too much like an expensive luncheonette.

anyway we went there and maybe it was a good idea, yes i'm sure it was. because a high class luncheonette is brightly lit and one cannot begin to weep all over again in a brightly lit luncheonette. maybe one on tenth avenue yes. but not one on central park south and not this one. so then it was what did i want and though it was may i was cold, was freezing cold so i ordered onion soup.

THE LOWER-WORKING-CLASS NARRATIVE OF A BLACK CHINESE AMERICAN GIRL

Wendy Thompson

I made my life from scratch. Built this twenty-two-year-old body from nothing. Just two wires and a burnt-out car, two pieces of tarp, and some scrap metal. And with these I built my bones, my skeleton, and my skin. A home to withstand sleet and rain, drunken assaults, and rape. A space to create beauty and dream, to leave a part of myself behind as artifact.

I came into this life carved out of poverty and half Blackness. Grew up on Lucky Charms and public-access television, I thought, like everybody else. I was cared for by my mother, an immigrant from Burma who shifted from Chinese restaurant waitress jobs to working as a baby sitter. I was punished by a Black father who came home tired and hungry from punching numbers at a shipping company on the Oakland waterfront.

My mother reminded me that it was her idea to wait in line overnight while pregnant with me back in the early '80s to try and get a loan from the bank to buy a house. She asserts (usually implying my father's failures) that without her, our family would be nothing. She wanted to make things work for herself and for her daughter. She needed to prove something to her family after getting kicked out and disowned for "going Black" and shaming the family name.

My African-American father grew up hard. He didn't hustle and was always intent on making money the "honest" way. He still had hope that this white man's world would be just, that they'd cut a little Black boy from San Francisco some slack. But he was angry and could not change the spiral of his own small life and stayed trapped in the menial-labor pool while his white coworkers got the raises and vacation time slots. All he got was some damn sweater with the company logo on it after twenty-plus years of "excellent service."

So this was my beginning, growing up in a lopsided house with my father's burnt-out anger and my mother's shaky dreams. We lived in Oakland between gunshots and freeway overpasses. My parents always had ambitions of making enough money to buy us out of the urban streets. Of course they wanted to give all three of us a nice little house with a picket fence and green grass to hide our abuse and sadness in. Not with nights of barricaded doors because a boy armed with a loaded weapon was loose in the neighborhood. Not with the neighbors across the street hosting gang parties and someone being fatally stabbed in a whirl of music and beer. Not with prostitution and a stabbing on the corner, a vague picture of a Black man being passed around as the suspect.

But this is the compromise—we were not white, we were not rich, we were not privileged. My mother couldn't speak English and my father was trying to swallow the whole of employment discrimination and a new family. In my own world, I was trying to save my skin from getting beaten up by classmates because of the poor Salvation Army clothes I wore or the way my half-breed awkwardness caused them to feel ill at ease. I got driven to the "good school" in the hills because my parents wanted the best for me. Not for me to break down at eleven and start fucking the neighborhood boys, getting drunk, and cutting school with a baby on the way. No, not that.

My mother wanted me to be a good little Asian daughter; my father wanted me to be able to escape the violence and dejection of growing up Black. They both wanted me to have a "chance" and make it in this world. So my father beat me to make me grow up tall and straight. My mother taught me to stay away from Blackness, to carefully construct myself so that I would not fuck up, and to hold it together until we reached the safety of suburbia and the middle class. Maybe, they thought, the whiteness would rub off on me. Maybe it would save me from cutting my arms with broken glass and running away with drunk homeless boyfriends.

But after all my father's efforts to beat me straight and my mother's insistence that I stop "acting ghetto" (read: an exaggerated performance of what I thought was Black), I ran away anyway. It wasn't the two-story house that I wanted so much, but this was beyond their comprehension.

Poverty and race, then, like stealing napkins from McDonald's for our own kitchen table or buying in bulk when my mother would steal from my father's tight wallet, were one and the same to me. I had grown up half Black and poor and had felt ashamed of myself and where I came from ever since I got thrown into schools with other kids who could afford to buy their social status. Those kids, the ones who were worth being called on, the milky White Rabbit candy–hands raised to a teacher's ambitious question. And the girls—from elementary to high school—always had the luxury of looking pretty, while I had only what I could afford, and even if I could afford it, would it ever be enough?

From this I became the unwanted, dusty half-breed girl from the other side of the tracks. I ate old food wrapped up in aluminum foil for lunch. Stinky food sometimes. Chinese food.

I do not know when I began to relate racism to whiteness, class and poverty to supremacy and economic/corporate tyranny, my family in the bottom of the curved belly of American lies. This kind of consciousness wasn't entirely mine at a young age since I lacked the framework and mental capacity to understand it all, but in the little ways that I could for-mulate it, I learned that I wielded a power and strength that these little Richie Rich kids would never have. They had all the privilege in the world, all the workings on their side, but I was still standing, still surviving after a thousand-year captivity that their world and their books constantly tried to erase from history, from memory and re-create as myth.

For so long, they—politicians, pastors, teachers, the three-car-garage rich—pushed the "pull yourself up by your bootstraps" theory. They said, "You Black people are so lazy. If you got off welfare and worked hard, maybe you could make something of yourselves in life."

But we Black people have been making something of ourselves in life, not only for ourselves but also for white people, for generations.

They never seem to hear us, though.

Being half Black means having thicker blood and bones to withstand breaking, and eyes with a raw, wide-open perspective. (Not all of us choose to live or see, but those of us who do know the difficulties of staying on top and navigating the currents of life.) Being poor is knowing how to make old milk and some bread go pretty far over the course of a week. Being a woman is learning from a young age what you can get in return for sex. So, my mother fed me on what she could make work, and what I didn't get from my parents, I received in exchange for my body, for all I was worth. And it isn't worth too much in this society, Blackness in the female form. Especially when you have to eat and have no skills, or are underage. *Blame it on history.*

For me, being half Black, poor, and troublesome somehow took the crime out of my rape and battery. It wasn't necessarily a legal issue that a young woman from *that side* was out in the streets getting beat up because she refused to give sex without some compensation. It wasn't a crime that she was being neglected in her home, it wasn't a crime that she went into the streets to look for an alternate family system. In that respect, I became a statistic, a government-study number, what talk-show hosts might call "a troubled girl looking for a father figure and love." But it wasn't severe enough for intervention when a young, poor woman who was labeled "gifted" by teachers in school but "mentally unstable" by psychiatrists was being battered and seeking alternatives—but found too many bricks instead that, in the end, created dead-end walls.

Still, I was literate. I loved English and my Anatomy class, even. And I stuck through school and graduated. During that time, I kept in my company a transient boyfriend who was also mixed-race but looked white, the same one who did the majority of the assaults on my body. My liberation came when he went away to boot camp the summer after senior year. At eighteen I was referred, as a "bright and qualified student," to college, and began yet another adjustment at the University of California at Santa Barbara, the U.C. notorious for being unable to keep students of color at the institution. It was a four-year fraternity party from which I bailed after just two years because of severe depression, alienation, and a climax of threatening to knuckle up with some of the white girls who constantly harassed me in the dorms.

I was not the first in my extended family to go away to college, but coming from an immediate family with a Chinese mother with minimal English skills and an African-American father who went to a city college and hit the glass ceiling hard, my attending a four-year university was not some minor thing. I transferred schools, determined to complete my bachelor's degree, unfinished with the fight.

I was still recovering from the earlier abuse, physical and mental, from boyfriends and other men. I was still trying to find my space to surface and not drown in academia, a place I was not totally prepared for after so many years in the California public school system, where I was channeled into underachieving classes because the school had already filled their "quota" for the honors courses. I was still cutting up my body periodically as my own way of coping, and would sometimes go out drinking to forget my difficulties. When I did study, I had to beg to borrow other kids' books because if I spent my financial aid money on the textbooks for my courses, I wouldn't be able to buy a Greyhound ticket back home to visit my family for the holidays.

I endured financially in school by depending on loans and painful budgeting. Even now, nothing for me is ever a luxury. I learned to stretch money and sometimes starve because something else is always much more important than food, something else always comes first. It's the sacrifice I have learned to live with while my mother supports the two younger additions to our family—two more girls—on minimum wage earned as a cashier at a fast-food restaurant. I used to be very ashamed to admit to people where she worked. Admitting these personal things can still remind me of the hurt I felt growing up poor and being made fun of.

It's our (brown) bodies that this society was built on and is still being built on, our backs, our hands still in the dirt. And it's easy for someone from outside this "class" to discredit the everyday struggle, simple for them to dissociate themselves from our shame, our labor, our humility, our anger. My mother has never been ashamed of who she is, even after her Chinese relatives cussed her out for going with a "nigger" and having half-breed babies without being able to support them. She fought to stand firm with her choices and stay proud of her work—owning a home and a car, helping one kid through college with two more to go. But what she does is regarded by American society as "nothing," a dirty shit job: mopping up someone else's floor and taking in their shame; probably even serving from a drive-through window some of the people who will read this book. Same as the work done by my father—refilling paper clips, photocopying papers, running Post-it note messages to court superiors—a "go get my coffee, boy." No one seems to notice that my parents, two underprivileged people, are doing the body work, the labor that keeps part of this world functioning.

Some of us survive, even as the world is caving in on us under the spread of capitalism and global industry. Some of us find new ways to pay the rent, pull together a family in a one-bedroom apartment, pay for an education with hope that a back will be spared—and hands too—while dealing with the persisting circumstances of poverty. There is a desire to close the gap between privileged and poor in this country, but it seems that regardless of the amount or quality of labor performed, the demarcations remain. The borders between the upper class and the working class stand to define more than just the amount on a paycheck. They classify language, culture, body, and self. It keeps us apart from each other while also keeping us connected in a never-ending struggle for social and economic balance. The middle ground is where I locate myself.

BLUEPRINTS AND HARDWIRES

Cassie Peterson

"Cassie, I want to know all of you . . . all the stories," she says naively over the phone. It's late at night and I'm cuddled into the receiver. I want to fulfill her request, but I'm scared she'll realize that's all I am—just a tangle of stories. I live these stories instead of a life. The motives get fuzzy.

Post–9/11. People stop buying sex toys. I know this only because I work at the very respectable sex store Good Vibrations. The co-op is cooperatively spooked. Everyone is talking about being "in the red." I imagine that people are still fucking, maybe even more. But it's a different kind of sex. More desperate, less methodical—back-alley blowjobs and hastened quickies. People fear war, the end of the world even. It makes them less inclined to purchase an eighty-dollar vibrator. I'm the new kid at the store—the first to be let go in the company's effort to survive the wintry economic climate.

It's like flatlining, losing your job. From thirty-five hours a week to zero. Zero hours. Zero structure. Zero dollars. I've been unemployed before, but it was always by choice. I was emotionally and financially pre- pared. But when someone else pulls the plug, it sends you reeling into the now empty seven days of your week. Anyone who's been laid off will tell you that it takes a full two weeks just to get out of your pajamas. You order a lot of take-out and watch a lot of *Maury Povich*. And then the money goes. And then you get dressed.

I am overwhelmed by the rigmarole of bureaucratic paperwork. I can't keep it all straight—the unemployment forms, the food-stamp applications, the drastically increasing number of ID cards that I am being forced to carry around with me. Being poor is a full-time job. Every minute, the government demands that you *prove* your current economic status, leaving absolutely no time to *improve* it. I have to schedule job interviews between all my other red-tape appointments.

I am in a three-hour line in the social services building. It's San Francisco's version of a Third World country—a desperate urban underbelly. I am surrounded by men right out of prison. Women with three kids and no home. Pregnant again. Shopping carts parked outside. Junkies going through withdrawal right here, they've been in line so long. I am filling out more forms. Always more forms. I use red pen, losing my patience and writing snide answers in the margins, like, "No, I have no new income to report. Don't you fucking get it? I'm broke. Just like yesterday and the day before." The man at the window is not amused. He shoots me a scolding look and hands me a fresh form to fill out. "Just mark the correct boxes," he warns.

I'm waiting for my number to be called with my head between my knees. It stinks in here like dirty feet. The woman next to me is nodding off, leaving her purse free for a swiping. I wonder if I should wake her. A guy in gold chains and slurred speech is passing his time by propositioning every woman in the waiting room. At one point I hear him say, "Hey, what can I say? I make really beautiful babies." The current object of his attention giggles into her hands. I scan the room. I am one of the only white people in here. I am suddenly self-conscious. Ashamed even, as if people are going to judge me because I have fallen from grace, from my privileged place in the social hierarchy. I walked into this waiting room from a world that most of these people have never had access to. This is only a moment for me— an excruciating moment, but still only a moment.

The top of my form reads, *Check here if this is not your reality. Sign on the dotted line if this is ultimately just another story for you to write.*

"Twenty-something white girl goes on government aid in order to find herself." How quaint. Later I will be able to flippantly say things like, "Oh, yeah, that was back when I was on food stamps." My revelations make me feel sad and heavy. Being here is sad. Being an outsider here is even sadder. I wrestle with the words. Poor. Poverty. I feel unequipped to attach myself to either. I'm "broke," which means now, not always. I have lived paycheck to paycheck for so long that I cannot even fathom another mode of existence. But it is still not poverty. I don't want to romanticize poverty by trying to apply it to my own life.

Today I have a job interview and then another meeting with my social worker. I try to clean up. God, I'm a mess. I don't have money for a haircut, so I'm deluding myself into thinking that I'm growing it out. My eyes are like two piss holes in the snow and my face is breaking out. I look damn near desperate. My interview is for a position as a basketball-camp facilitator at the Stonestown YMCA. The program director meets with me. Her name is Susan. She's from Florida and wears a long, pink cardigan sweater. She's a writer too, she informs me. Everyone in San Francisco is a writer. We're like locusts. "Wow, what a coincidence!" I say with impeccable enthusiasm.

She leads me to her office and I'm ready to dazzle her with the vastness of my basketball experience. But first she asks about my last job. Shit, I didn't work that one into the equation. I think of as many euphemisms for Good Vibrations as I possibly can. I downplay sex and highlight customer service and diversity training. She's visibly unimpressed. I get nervous and suddenly feel less qualified. I fidget with my tie while Susan glares at it, as if it's some intrusive third party. I am subtly indicted for being some kind of creepy, tie-wearing child molester. Wow, this is not going well. I've never had a bad interview before and suddenly I'm feeling really defeated.

Susan feeds me some scenarios. "What would you do if one of the kids in your group needs to use the restroom and you are the only adult on the premises?" I think hard. Then it hits me like a jackpot. My eyes light up and I explain how I would utilize the buddy system. But it's not quick enough for her. She wants those kinds of answers to shoot out of me like bullets from a machine gun. There's plenty of people who have that child-care lingo crap cued up and ready to go. I just really like basketball. "Do you have CPR certification?"

"Well, no," I say, "but I'd be willing to take some sort of class, and did I mention that I've been playing basketball for as long as I can remember?"

"*Mm hmm.*" She then asks me what I would do if one of the kids were misbehaving.

"I'd tell that little fuck to shape up!" I say assertively. Well, O.K., I didn't actually say that. But I think that's what Susan heard. By this point, we're just going through the motions. I shake her hand and exhale away all my discomfort. Back on the Muni train, I wedge myself in between droves of S.F. State kids. They are fresh out of their film classes. They all look the same—kind of washed out. They wear pins on their jean jackets and talk about sustainable agriculture. I wince at how predictable it all is.

I'm sitting in Clara's cubicle. She's my social worker. She is friendly, but keeps it strictly professional. I like her because she helps me and I don't feel shamed by it. We meet weekly. She always asks, "What are your plans?" I never know. But today I attempt an answer. "Maybe I should go back to school. Or maybe I'll just move to a different city and start over."

"O.K., but you will no longer be eligible for any California state aid if you do either of those things."

"I know," I say. "I was just musing."

"Don't muse in here," she warns. "I've got twenty more people to see before lunch." I relinquish yet another signature and a full set of fingerprints. "California officially owns you," she informs me.

Tuesday night. I stroll into the Lexington bar, city-dyke central. We all look the same—card-carrying members of some incestuous social network. If you put in the time, you gain access to all the perks. It's like a pyramid scheme. I've been involved for about two years and I've dated every cute, brown-haired, andro, five-foot-something dyke in the city. I must have filled out a profile card or something because they get delivered to my front doorstep with thirty-day warranties. But the sacrifice is incredible sometimes. Like tonight. I promised I would show up, despite my own good sense not to. I've been extremely reclusive since my quality of life started rapidly deteriorating, but I got a phone call. People are worried. I'm nursing a beer in the corner, fighting off feelings of dread. I've had such a long day, I don't know if I can play the part right now. But if I don't, people might suspect that I've been busy living my own life, in my own skin, and I don't want to alienate anyone like that. No, no, I'm here, sucking off the generic group battery. But tonight, it feels like one of those 9-volts that shock you when you put it to your tongue.

One of my buddies shows up. She comments on the startling length of my hair. "I know, I know," I say as I blow it out of my face. She updates me on all the gossip as the bar fills up. I watch her eyes. I watch everyone's eyes. They're in constant motion. Everyone in the bar is looking through everyone else, hoping to see something new. Something better. We're always upgrading. I feel raw—everything right at the surface. I'm ready to climb atop a soapbox and condemn the entire thing—the patterns of behavior we establish under the guise of "creating community." This isn't community. Communities support each other. Communities look each other in the eyes. I feel most angered by my own part in it all. It's just so easy, so comfortable, so . . . inexcusable.

"How are you?" my friend finally says.

"Honestly?" I ask.

"Of course," she says earnestly, oblivious to what's brewing under my social veneer.

"I'm scared I'm not going to be able to pay rent this month. I'm scared that I'm losing everything."

"Well, can't your dad just send you some money?" I'm tempted to hit her, just to shake her loose from her own sense of entitlement. She is near-sighted from too many years of having everything she wants.

"Dude, my dad makes less money than I do," I try to say politely. Another story is tickling the back of my throat. It's a soliloquy really, so I move to the corner of the stage and address my audience. "I can't just count on some familial rescue. I'm sorry that didn't occur to you. I'm sorry that I am suddenly too messy to fit into your one-dimensional version of me."

I'm back in Wyoming. High school. My father and I are fighting about money. He teaches creative writing courses at the local college, but he keeps his hours to a minimum so that he can devote more time to his own writing. Our whole life is lived at the bare minimum. "Why can't you just get a real job?" I scream maliciously. "Why don't you just stop whining and work for once in your life?" He recoils. I've just pulled the trigger on the weapon that he's had to protect himself from his whole life. He's gotten it from all directions. His dad, my mother, and now me. He starts to cry, right there. He's a fifteen-year-old boy, fascinated with Ezra Pound, wondering why nobody understands him. "I'm sorry, Dad, I didn't mean it."

I picture him as a real Wyoming dad. He's an engineer in the coal mines. He drives a truck with a shotgun in the back. He silently caves into his recliner after a ten-hour shift and drinks Budweiser. I shudder to think. "I mean it—I'm really sorry. It's just so hard with you sometimes."

The story runs its course and I get up from the bar. I cannot be here anymore. I am clearly spilling outside the lines of the identity that affords me a comfortable place here. I'm hiding from ideas that loom in the sky like mushroom clouds. Stalking around my neighborhood in nondescript hats and sunglasses, I am aching for total invisibility.

I'm headed toward the Mission Library. I need to check Craig's List for more job openings, but I panic as I approach Valencia. I can't even get near that street without feeling like I'm in an episode of *This Is Your Life*. There is a constant barrage of familiar faces. A black car is approaching and it looks just like it belongs to someone I know. I spook like a jackrabbit and hop into a thorny row of bushes. The car passes and it's not her. A wave of sanity washes over me, as I become aware of myself on all fours in branches that are scraping the skin off my knees. There is nothing left to do but laugh. I make it home unnoticed. My unemployment check has come. It's a joke, of course, since they have based the amount on some old job I used to have before I was paying rent in the city. I pay my phone bill before I no longer have the resources to do so. There's an envelope from my dad. It's a check for thirty dollars and a note that says, "Cass, I am thinking about you all the time. Sorry this is all I could afford, as things are pretty tight here as well." It breaks his heart to send it. And mine to endorse it.

Using my food stamps in the grocery store reminds me of buying tampons in Wyoming. There is a great deal of self-consciousness involved. In my town, there is only one store, so there was never any possibility of anonymity. Inevitably all my teachers and crushes were in the same checkout line with me. The kid bagging groceries was always some awkward teenage boy I knew from geometry class. He put his grubby hands all over my box of supers. The next day at school he'd shoot me a chilling look that said, "I know about you. You're the one who *bleeeeds.*"

Alone now, standing in the Cala checkout line in the middle of the night in order to feel less conspicuous, the implications feel far more serious. I'm being rung up by a middle-aged man with a grocery-clerk mustache. I need him to walk me through this, so I confess, "I've never done this before." I hand him a wad of pink and blue money, shaking. I feel compelled to explain my circumstances to him. "I lost my job, but don't worry, I'm fine. Everything's fine. I promise."

Through the receiver, she's telling me a story this time. More like an anecdote. The punch line is something about how this morning she was wearing Puma shoes with a red button-down shirt and the combo made her feel too sporty or euro or euro-sporty. But it's O.K. now, because she went home after work and changed her shoes. She really dodged a faux pas fashion bullet. I've tuned out. I just nod in agreement instead of saying, "I'm sorry, but I really don't give a fuck."

And just like that, it's the first line of a brand-new story. It's unraveling. I can tell it's going to be climactic by the heat it creates in my belly. I'm completely present in the spaces between the words. It hits me—this is the big scare. This is what everyone warned me about when I was growing up. Having nothing. Losing everything. We learn how to be financially secure, socially well adjusted. We go to school and collect degrees and hoard everything around us so that we can get further and further from the very place where I am sitting. I am drenched in a pool of my own exhilaration. I am en route, aware that this is possibly the worst time of my entire life, while simultaneously understanding that I have never been more alive. It's like being seven years old and everything around you is vibrating with possibility.

"I'm living really close to things," I suddenly offer up to her.

"What do you mean?" She has obviously not been reading my mind. I wish I could show her everything I've seen. I want to air-drop her into the middle of a previous paragraph. There's a time capsule buried under my numbness and it's resurfacing. In it are all the old blueprints and hard-wires. I remember again what it's like to have no other purpose than to survive. I'm free and comforted here. She's waiting patiently to be let in, but I still struggle to drop all the pretenses. "You know, vanity . . . it's such a stifling luxury." Great, now I'm speaking to her in aphorisms. Without any context, she's not going to buy into this.

"Thanks, Dad," she scoffs.

I deserve that. It's no secret I'm withholding. I finally just say it. "Right now, nothing matters. I'm not cute or charming. I'm not a storyteller or a writer. I'm wearing dirty underwear . . . again. I'm a mere number in a per-petual shuffle of human need. And the good days are the ones where I remember that."

She hears me, and that is all I can ask for.

THE SOUND OF POVERTY

Eileen Myles

When I think about the type of poverty I grew up with I'm inclined to call it "enough." We had just enough. I guess we were what they call now the working poor. We weren't really poor, but my parents were afraid of that—poverty. So there were many actions and choices in between us and poverty and we lived in that in-between place where you were always slightly reminded that you didn't have enough or you had barely enough.

I always think of the powdered milk. What kid didn't like to drink milk, tons of it—a half gallon was plunked down on the table at supper and at lunch. But sometimes my mother sank down a pitcher and there were tiny bubbles at the top of it and we'd scream: No, Mom, it has bubbles. It's powdered! It's not, she'd insist. Then she'd give in. O.K., she'd admit. It's half and half. Everything was always getting stretched a little bit. At a moment when everyone was proudly aware of the pop glamour of American products, we didn't use Welch's grape jelly—we used Ann Page, the A&P brand. Or Finast from First National. When it came to ice cream it was Marvel, whatever that was, and it was also neapolitan so that nobody could have their favorite flavor, everybody could have striped ice cream or nothing. Neapolitan is strawberry, vanilla, and chocolate. You probably know that. We didn't have Kool-Aid, we had Cheeri-ade, our supermarket's brand. I loved when we ran out of something just before

supper because I'd jump on my bike and go to the Monument market in
the center which was run by some Italian guy who wore a straw hat and
the Monument only carried brand names, we were locked in to something
known. But usually we weren't. As a result, there were certain things that
actually seemed disgusting to me. Like butter. Too rich. I preferred margarine. I had to develop a taste for butter in college so that I wouldn't
embarrass myself by my preference for blandness. I'm afraid to taste margarine now because I think I would still like it too much and I would think
about home. Growing up poor—growing up anything other than middle
class situates you strangely in the culture. For instance, I don't like television. Unlike every middle-class girlfriend I've ever had, I watched it plenty
growing up. No one ever stopped me. Also, it was the sixties. TV was like
a national sport. Those people who were questioning whether it was good
for kids were total outsiders. Conceited and rich. Probably the same
people who were willing to put their entire family on TV, like the Louds.
My family would eat supper and then my mother would make about three
dozen chocolate-chip cookies and we'd watch TV until it went off. We'd
watch Johnny Carson and then we'd watch American jets fly over
Buddhist temples and "The Star Spangled Banner" would play and we'd
call it a day. Nobody did homework. Nobody asked. There was no future.
We were just there. My brother was considered a brain and he got good
grades somehow and I didn't but it didn't matter, because I was a girl. So
right from the beginning it seemed that being female was another occasion of poverty. In fact there were two of us in my family. We were referred
to as "the girls." Immediately I was part of a group. It's been pointed out
to me that in photography kids of color are generally photographed in
groups rather than in individual portraits like white kids. In general, it
seems to me, girls are less white than boys, or white in the wrong way. And
again, there were two of us, so the more, the worse. And I was more a part
of the group of my family than the group at school. My family was kind of
Old-World. If all the females were getting permanents, I would get a permanent. There was no personal self, no point of resistance. Whatever style
was tearing through the legions of other girls at school had no effect on
the fashions of my family. Since there were two girls we would often get

the same thing: two dresses, identical. My brother was a little different from us. There was the sense that he would go to a brand-name college, and my mother helped him buy a car in high school—a Volkswagen; yet still in the most basic ways he was just like us. He watched TV and he went to bed. He got up and the jelly and the margarine were there and—let me show you our lunch boxes. It was cool to have your sandwich on a big bulky roll—but of course instead I had Wonder Bread—oddly one of the brands that broke through to the working class. Everyone had it. I think Wonder Bread was considered good because of all those ways it built the body and it was also great to have a Drake's cake in your lunch box, but I did not have a Drake's cake, I had an apple with a bruise. It's better for you, my mother would defend it. And she was right. But still I couldn't believe those lucky kids would open their boxes or their bags and a product in cellophane would gleam out at them. And they would tear it open and the whipped cream would be stuck to the paper and it was theirs.

In school there was a band. I dreamed about it—a marching band with drums and clarinets and saxophones—the best. I desperately wanted to join the band and play music with everyone. But my mother simply said no. We couldn't afford it. My brother had a paper route so he could afford it, but Terry didn't practice. Why would my mother waste the money on a horn I wouldn't play, she explained snootily. She actually had distaste for the idea. But I would, I believed, my hopes fading into the wallpapered walls of our two-family house that we owned. See, we weren't poor. We were World War II white average. My parents bought our house on the G.I. bill. Obviously other guys went to college on it as well. Not my father. My father decided to drink himself to death and die instead. When we wanted something my mother would immediately compare her experience—orphan, to our experience—lucky ducks with two parents, and then even one. It was easy to say no to me. She would think of what she had had—what they had taken away from her. At the point at which both of her parents died, there was a pianola in her house and she believed it was hers and the Polish relatives came and carted it away. People take everything. That's what my mother believed. I think we kids were "people" too. By the time I was eleven and had given up the possibility of ever playing the trumpet, or the clarinet or the saxophone, and merely sat on a chair in the parlor tooting on my harmonica, my mother would lean in and say, You know, I always wanted to play the piano when I was a child. She looked at me sadly. We were a couple of kids. So it's really difficult when I think about growing up without money, not much of it anyhow—to figure out what in fact was the weirdness of our exact economic situation and what was the kind of mourning that people endlessly express through dollars. My mother couldn't let me replace her loss with a living kid with a horn. I had to stay empty too. And I did. I really think of language as a replacement for everything. Sitting here at my computer it's like the revenge of nothing. I make my constant claim in silence. I toot my horn.

DIRTY GIRL

Tara Hardy

"When the ax came into the forest, the trees said the handle is one of us."

—bumper sticker

The dispute between femmes and feminists is about class. We get stuck with one another because we disagree about which practices feed, or are born of, the patriarchy. Feminists judge femmes from the perspective of class.

My personal experience with feminists has been complicated. One of the complications involves how quickly feminists attempt to snatch the ideals they espouse out of my hands when I apply them to my right to express femininity. I get asked a lot by feminists, either out loud or with the nonverbal once-over, "Why are you wearing that skirt, that make-up, those shoes?" More than once someone has actually said out loud, "I thought you were a feminist." When this happens, I pause to think about my aunts and cousins, my hometown friends who still don't look like the girls at college did when I got there. I remember that at one point, neither did I. And what I want to say is, "Because I'm homesick."

In spite of what anyone might think about the whys and ways of femininity, I have to be honest: I don't feel cleaner when I'm unadorned, scrubbed, uncovered. I feel dirty and ungendered. I feel like the animal of reproduction I was meant to be as a working-class woman, existing to spawn the next crop of sturdy workers. Girls like me were born to labor, not to have sexualities—except maybe as farm animals. We were raised to service the landowner without question or compensation. We were also raised to service the landowner's wife, so she could remain unsmudged, uncalloused, and monochromatically pale.

In response to the above, as an act of resistance, my working, nonconsensually degendered ancestors created a sexuality, a femininity, that is loud and unmistakable. It's offensive to your middle-class sensibilities because it's supposed to be.

The logic of wishing I'd just lay down my femininity and stop fouling up the feminist movement is flawed. Our definitions of liberation, of revolution, profoundly differ. Calling me a tool of the patriarchy does nothing but objectify me. The real tool is shaming the working class—patriarchy doesn't swing just on sexism, but on all kinds of oppression: classism, racism, ageism, and ableism, to name a few. And because our locations on the map of oppression differ from one another, so too will our definitions of gender liberation.

But they keep asking. These feminists, these daughters of lawyers, professors, engineers, and doctors ask me, incredulously, why I think they're the enemy. Here's why.

When I was eight, my pediatrician found evidence of my father sexually abusing me. My vagina was growing together where the friction from him was leaving it raw. It was growing together to keep him out. Instead of reporting it, the doctor told my mother I wasn't washing properly. He said I was dirty. That's when he put his thumbs on either side of my vagina and yanked me apart.

To him, I wasn't worth saving. None of us were. To him, we were all dirty, despite showering with Dial every day. Having watched television, we'd taken its advice for how to get clean. The doctor approved—he prescribed Dial soap in the wound every day, followed by Vaseline. There were child-abuse laws in 1972. But it was easier for the doctor to call my family dirty, to send me home diagnosed "unclean" instead of "raped."

The intersection of class with this horrible moment is what puts me over the edge. I've successfully lived through the pain, the tearing, the hot throb of tender skin—I'm still living through "dirty." When I should have been wrapped in tissue paper and hurried to safety, I was, instead, stamped: Filth.

In addition to class, race collides with this moment. Because if we hadn't been white, parental rights would more likely have been swiftly snipped. I'm under no illusion that I would have been escorted to safety; rather, I would have been raped, dirty, *and* stolen—a modern echo of an earlier practice. But I know my father, at least in part, got to keep me because he's white. I don't think I would have benefited from being taken away, but I do think I would have benefited from the doctor doing the work necessary to intervene in my small life.

In 1972, women were being "liberated." When my father lost the only real job he'd ever had, organizing for the United Auto Workers, my mother had the "privilege" of putting her infant, my brother, into day care and going to work. Unlike the women in the suburbs who could choose the age at which they'd leave their children nestled with nannies in their comfortable homes, for my mother, being liberated did not mean the "opportunity" to get a job. For her, true choice would have meant the option to stay home with her new baby without having to wean him. At first, my mother tried to make it to the baby sitter's during her breaks, but my brother was too hungry in between. Left no other choice, she spent night after night rocking him back and forth, trying to get her desperate baby to take the bottle. She was desperate herself by the time he finally did. During all of this, I was desperately home alone with my father.

So, excuse me for not trusting the feminists. For not trusting the bourgeois movement of those with enough time on their hands to actually feel dissatisfied. My mother didn't have time for dissatisfaction—she had time for labor. Far from being fulfilled at her job, she was imprisoned by it. And so, by association, was I. We were trapped, at least in part, because I wasn't clean enough to be saved, and because my mother's labor wasn't valuable enough to be paid properly. "Equal pay for equal work" means between men and women doing similar jobs, laborers or not. What equal pay for equal work should mean is the same wage for an *hour*—pushing a broom, pushing art, pushing pills, or pushing around money.

What galls me is that the modern-day offspring of the feminists who coined the "equal pay" phrase in the first place are still calling me dirty— in much more sophisticated terms, but still dirty. What it sounds like today is accusations of my expressing an abhorrent "traditional femininity." What I have to say about that is, Check your traditions.

Some of us who are claiming what has been mistaken as "traditional femininity" are doing so precisely because it was *not* part of our cultural or familial traditions. Those of us who aren't middle/upper/owning class, who don't wear suits or don pearls with our New York haircuts, and who haven't had the privilege to buy our genders at fucking Nordstrom. Those of us who have cleaned other people's shit off their walls, and I'm not speaking metaphorically here, in exchange for a wage that forces us to ruin that ledger of moral character known as the "credit rating," because we can't afford the cost of living and have the gall to need a phone, heat, or a pair of goddamned shoes anyway. It would also include those of us whose mothers could not afford the latest understated, tasteful, college-bound tweed skirt and penny loafers. Not to mention the notebook filled with aspirations that you really *can* be what you want to be when you grow up, that even if you slip up, you'll be welcomed back into the fold and not labeled "slut" forever.

It is on purpose that I am rejecting your guidelines for femininity. Let me say that again—it is precisely your ruling-class, understated femininity I'm rejecting. Your subtle, no-one-would-mistake-me-for-a-slut-even-though-I-might-be-a-bad-girl-in-secret femininity. (By the way, we all know those boarding school girls have been giving as many blowjobs as we have.)

I don't think it's any kind of coincidence that rich girls and feminists all look so scrubbed. Which is not to say I don't believe in working-class feminism. But a caution to any feminist: If what you're doing is making the dirty girls ashamed of ourselves, then whose agenda are you really fulfilling? If what you're doing is making you look back at your poor, duped, uneducated ancestors and think they're stupid, I challenge you to look deeper at their ways of resisting. Because I'm not so arrogant as to reject their traditions of resistance, I'll just keep whacking off my leg hair and painting myself with loud lipstick and putting on bright colors. I will not be a pale, muted thing to serve anyone else's idea of "liberation."

I've had lots of conversations with educated women about things like the "dominant discourse" regarding shaving, in which I struggle to come up with language to defend my choices about my own body. (Is anyone missing the irony of respecting my right to choose whether or not to reproduce, but not whether or not to shave?) During these conversations, I find myself translating my arguments into a tongue that is not my primary language. I am expected—as are other women like me—to come up with a perfectly justifiable argument. But there's no recognition for what's being lost in translation. Nervously, I'll say something like, "Acknowledging the dominant discourse about shaving, I still hold that I'm not giving in to the patriarchy by removing the hair from my legs. Rather, I'm honoring the tradition of gender expression that has been passed on to me by my ancestors." A sentence I'm capable of constructing, at least in part, because I went to college. But in my original tongue, this same sentiment might sound something like this: "Whatever. Fuck that. I get to shave if I want to. My mother raised me to do it, and it makes me feel like a girl."

I recently had a conversation with a middle-class, feminine, queer friend who's getting her law degree. She had her first day in court, and while there was much to report, she zeroed in on the court clerk, who was wearing a shimmering silver top with a too-short skirt and "way too much make-up." My friend thought she made the courtroom look "unprofessional." This is the same friend who's offered to show me how to put on make-up that doesn't look like you're wearing it—my thought is, What the hell for? If I go to the effort, do I want it to be invisible? I guess that's what she wanted from the clerk—invisibility, or to "blend," as they say.

My question is this: Does it ever occur to the privileged that we don't actually want to emulate you? My god, the staggering arrogance! Does it ever occur to you that we think *you're* filthy? And maybe, just maybe, we don't ever want to be mistaken for one of you?

As queers, we know this argument for why we look different. We know it from defending ourselves from the line of questioning that goes, Why are you so tattooed, shorn, "alternative"? What I'm advocating is that we broaden the meaning of "alternative," that we recognize the "outside" that is the everyday for working people. I'm talking about those who, by any means necessary, get their children fed. When it comes to a working-class, outsider femininity, I think of *Erin Brockovich*. Although believing Julia Roberts as working-class is a little beyond me, when Erin is asked, in the film, "What makes you think you can just waltz in there and get [such incriminating evidence]?" she replies, "They're called boobs."

Once, when my butch lover was sick, we went to the emergency room for a visit we never intended to pay for—not because we'd spent all our money on partying, but because it was a cold winter and we needed the heat more than our credit rating. My lover needed an expensive antibiotic; the cheap ones had failed to clear up the infection in her lungs. The doctor wrote the prescription and instructed us to fill it at the hospital pharmacy. Faced with the knowledge that her infection was likely to get worse, I did a little "leaning" over the counter, and the doctor "found" some samples.

From that moment on, my lover took up the habit of asking me, "Baby, will you go in and lean?" when we badly needed something we couldn't afford. Sometimes it worked, sometimes it didn't. But this is precisely the kind of femininity I was taught to use to defend my loved ones.

A few months ago I was touring with a rogue band of poets and rap artists. In Las Vegas we were booked at a biker bar, most of whose patrons talked over us—poetry, I guess, not being their favorite form of entertainment. While one of the performers was on stage, he was verbally assaulted and physically intimidated by one of the bar's drunk, male patrons. The guy called him a "faggot" and threatened him. When it started, immediately, the feminine dykes were on our feet—our bodies in between the threat and the person we loved on stage. The harasser didn't stop right away, but he eventually did back down.

I think he backed down for a number of reasons. One, he was more reluctant to hit girls. (We knew this, which is why we put ourselves in the way. But, for the record, if it had come to it, none of us would have hesitated to fight back.) Two, he backed down because we were speaking working-class, a language he understood—fuck with someone we love, and you'll get swarmed. Three, he backed down because none of the masculine-identified people confronted him, so he didn't have to defend his masculinity. In my opinion, this was a case where sending in the girls was the most effective thing we could have done.

Later, when I said something to one of the dykes who'd leapt to her feet about the power of femininity, her response was, "Yeah, it made me sick to sell out like that; he should have backed down when Vinnie asked him to." She was right, he should have. But her comment also broke my heart. First, I don't think I, or any of us, were selling out our queerness, our loved one, or our femininity. We were being strong. It was a moment in which femininity could be seen for the bad-ass weapon it truly is.

I'm still not sure how to bridge the gap of silence between my friend and me, which grew from that point. I wonder now if she thinks my "brand" of femininity is dangerous to her. Although I'm familiar with what the feminist response would be, I want to tell her it was chicks and our chick-ness that defused that situation. Instead, I'm left feeling, somehow, that the distance between us means the patriarchy wins.

The instant—and I mean instant—I heard the term "femme," I started making sense to myself. It was 1987, I was standing in Connie and Cheryl's kitchen, and one of their rugby friends said to me, "You can't be a dyke, you don't look like one." Someone else said, "Tara? She's a femme." She was standing behind me and to the right, about six feet away, right by the jade plant.

I swiveled instantly and asked, "What? I'm a what?"

"A femme," she answered. The rest of them laughed.

Regardless of their laughter, that was the first time I knew there was a name for me. Which brings me to labels. While labels feel constricting for some, they've been liberating for me. Years after hearing the term "femme" for the first time, when I found what little has been written about our precious and vast femme history, I found this to be true: Femme is the keyhole I put my life into and turn, my experiences finally making sense. How many butch or androgynous girlfriends have I had who heard "lezzie" on the playground and knew it was what they were? Language can be used to oppress, but it can also liberate.

People will say that times have changed since that day in the kitchen. And they have—femmes are organizing, talking, writing our histories down. But they haven't changed all that much. I challenge you to wear a short skirt (not as a joke, but seriously) to the next dyke march. Wear that sucker down the street, on a bus, all day at work—see what it takes to sport femininity in the world.

Some of you will ask, if it's so much trouble, why wear it in the first place? And my answer is, Because it's as important to who I am, to honoring my gender, as your piercings, work boots, tattoos, or tie are to you. Because my brash femininity is the cornerstone of my resistance to a history that would have had me sexless except for reproduction.

This brings me, reluctantly, to urban hip fashion as a frequent co-optation of working-class culture. I've become beyond sick of the fashionably downwardly mobile who constantly treat us as theater. Donning the isn't-it-ironic, tongue-in-cheek gas station attendant jacket, formerly owned by the person whose name appears on the patch. Who just last week checked your oil, and you should have been ashamed to wear that thing in front of him. Please, take that jacket off, along with whatever else you're co-opting from the working class, and your—unless you have a cultural claim to them—tribal tattoos, fake bindis, and rearview-mirror dreamcatchers. Go ahead and return that sacred cloth you use as your curtain to its rightful owner, and unlock your hair unless you understand "dread" to mean something other than what you feel if the cops drive by when you're toting weed.

Many people in my town have long sported cool by wearing shirts that say "Mac" or "Joe" on labels sewn by someone's loving partner (could have been my cousin). The inception of this practice coincided with scores of people claiming trans identities and searching for masculine markers. While I celebrate such flagging, such external clues of internal identities, I'd like to caution us to be careful about whose masculinity we're adopting, and to ask ourselves whether we have a right to it. Working-class masculinity has long been sexualized by the upper classes, so it's no wonder that in modern-day gender fuck we find it so appealing. But the person who wore it before you is not a fashion wet nurse to be suckled by those hungry for cool.

A few final words for the feminists: I'm not asking you to paint yourselves, raise your hems, or shave off what your hair means to you. I am asking that you stand beside me fighting for my right to do so. My resistance doesn't look like yours. It never has. So create what you want, but know where it comes from. I do. Because the landowners made a mistake—they let us read. But not without being forced to. Remember the labor movement? Without it I'd be wasting away with my aunts on the Chevy, Ford, or Pontiac lines, which, maybe you didn't know, were modeled after slaughterhouses. Instead, I am here, using old tools in new ways. Because the new way is in our heads, in our powers of redefinition. I challenge you to try it. Otherwise what kinds of traditions are you breaking? Trying to make the dirty girls ashamed of ourselves isn't one of them.

Your label of "traditional"—I reject it. Because I'm not so arrogant as to reject the ways of resisting my ancestors fashioned, I'll just keep whacking off my leg hair, whether or not it's all right with you, and smearing my lips with loud lipstick. You see, I've inherited it, this fine tradition of resistance.

DINNER TALK

Liliana Hernández

At my house growing up, dinner wasn't a fancy social gathering to discuss politics or religion. Food provided the occasion to gossip about the neighbors, the women at my mom's factory, and Latina celebrities. Living in northern New Jersey with immigrant parents, I learned the hard way to be thankful for having a stocked refrigerator. Whenever I told Mami that I did not want any more of my dinner, she would say, "And with so many poor kids going hungry in Colombia! How can Americans waste so much food? Shameful!"

Food was part of our American dream: Levi's jeans, trips to New York, a thirty-year mortgage for a small old house with a yard, and red meat every day.

The afternoons of my childhood had a rhythm centered on food. I would come home from school, eat a snack, do my math homework, and then eat dinner. My snacks were processed: Cheetos, Doritos, or salty popcorn. Anything that crackled in my mouth and came in a twenty-five-cent bag. I also drank plenty of soda and fruit punch. Orange soda was my favorite, because it tasted like carbonated orange juice. I couldn't stand the homemade natural fruit juices my mother made, filled with pulp and strawberry seeds. They just wouldn't go down nice and smooth the way a Sunny Delight would. My diet was high in sugar, high in fat—but low on Mami's wallet.

My mom would get home around five. She would heat up food for my dad, who worked the night shift at the factory. He ate white rice with black beans and pork chops for dinner. Then my mother would quickly sit down to eat herself. She had double meals. First she would have chicken noodle soup straight out of the box, with some extra vegetables. Then she ate rice, beans, and pork, and whatever other leftovers my father did not eat. I was last on the food chain, whenever Mami was done.

My mother was never fond of cooking, although she liked the idea of having food around. We had no cookbooks in my house, only the Food Network. (Mami ordered basic cable to watch other people making gourmet meals.) My mother would watch the cooking shows and express amazement at their skill in slicing onions so fast, but she never tried new techniques. Cooking was more about opening a can or letting meat defrost than it was about preparing elaborate dishes like beef Wellington or rack of lamb with mint jelly and creamed onions. Mami's food was warm and generous, seasoned with her special sauce and love. The six most common meals at my house were *arroz con frijoles negros y chuleta* (rice with black beans and pork), *arroz con frijoles rojos y picadillo y maduros* (rice with red beans, meat, and fried plantains), *arroz con carne y papa* (rice with beef and potatoes), *tortillas,* Ellios pizza, and chicken tenders.

It is hard to look back and describe the taste of that food. We never talked about how soft and moist the rice was, what herbs seasoned the beef, or even what type of meat we were eating. Rice and beans with meat was the basic meal. The rice was soft and just moist enough. There were fat red pinto beans or pork-flavored black beans. There was always rice, and we made sure of it by purchasing twenty-pound bags of Carolina. We ate a lot of ground beef, seasoned with Mami's special sauce made of tomato paste, pepper, garlic, and onions. Having meat every day was a testament to living in the United States and not being poor. My father criticized people with big houses and leather couches who kept no meat in the fridge. They were not truly enjoying life. For him, to eat meat every day was to enjoy the finer things in life.

Vegetables were not part of the program, and my mom never mastered the art of making mashed potatoes. There were no side dishes, except for an occasional corn on the cob or baked potato. Mami would eat a salad of tomatoes, lettuce, cucumbers, and avocado, which she also urged me to eat, but no one ever really forced it upon me. I took Flintstone vitamins instead.

We rarely all sat down for dinner at the same time, in the same room, with the same meal, to converse. Since my dad and my sister worked nights, it was just Mami and me. Mami would tell me about the mean forewoman at work, who had no clue about sewing but bossed everyone around. She would tell me about how Fulana's daughter got pregnant and dropped out of high school. But most often, dinner was me eating in the living room, watching one of my favorite prime-time shows. It was by watching these shows that I learned how others (read: white middle-class people) ate dinner. They ate three-course meals with vegetables, meat, and dessert. Children passed their parents the mashed potatoes and said things like "thank you." The parents asked the children about what they had learned in school, and if they had a big test coming up. Then the mother would bring out dessert.

My mother never asked me about my day at school. I did not take this to mean that she did not care about me, but rather to mean that life was monotonous and rather uneventful. I never asked them about their factory work, if they had sewn sweaters or pants that day. Instead we talked about the real *telenovelas*—dramas in the lives of people around us. There was no passing of potatoes or being polite, and there were never people over for dinner.

Then came college.

I attended an all-women's college, where dinners involved complicated conversations about sex, politics, family, and past experiences. We talked about welfare reform, and whether we were for or against the World Trade Organization. But not only did the talk change from what I knew at home, the food was like nothing I had ever known: fettuccine with Alfredo sauce, shepherd's pie, lemon chicken, bowtie pasta with marinara sauce, turkey wild-rice casserole—wild! I soon realized that the change really mostly came down to the adjectives, while the food itself was, on the whole, the same. I had eaten chicken before but not lemon chicken, sauce but not Alfredo, and the rice back home was never wild. These meals were more like the ones I saw on TV, with foods that were topped with spices and herbs. They had creamy sauces that would slither on my tongue. I could taste the combination of lemon and parsley on the chicken. I enjoyed the filo dough crust of the shepherd's pie, stuffed with ground beef and vegetables.

Dessert was my favorite. At Smith College, I would do anything for a piece of dessert. I loved strawberry New York–style cheesecake, brownies showered with pecans and walnuts. We also could make our own ice cream sundaes by mixing sweet hot fudge and sticky caramel sauce on vanilla ice cream, with cherries on top. At the Friday teas there was escargot, but I would skip that and eat instead the homemade, soft, warm-from-the-oven M&M chocolate-chip cookies and brownies.

In college, there were so many options. Dessert at every meal was no longer a luxury, but the normal closing to our conversations. From talk about movies and MTV to in-depth discussions of social reform, my dinners in college gave me insight into other people's perspectives about the world and their homes. My college friends were white, middle-class, and from all fifty states. Some were raised in cities and others on farms with their own horses. It was nothing like my home. I figured Latinos just never ate like white college kids. That is, until I spent a semester in Chile.

I was the host student of a married couple. She worked for the university's online library; he was a retired engineer. Having been raised in an immigrant working-class small town, I had never met Latinos like this before. Dinners were even more different than at Smith. Suddenly I was living on the seventh floor of an apartment building with twenty-four-hour doorman security, my own bathroom, a patio, a twice-a-week maid, a living room with no television, and cultured host parents. Being a minority in the United States meant that I identified with the maids, mechanics, and servicemen. My parents constantly told me that nothing good ever came from Latin America. They did not understand my desire to go there, since I would surely see only poverty. Boy, were they wrong!

What I found with my host family were Latinos who had graduated from college and knew about Western culture—arts, literature, jazz, and social movements. My parents had not finished high school. They knew social movements to be protests, riots, or wars in Latin America—followed by higher prices for milk and eggs at *la bodega*.

Having dinner with my host family in Chile was very different. The menu might consist of turkey with wine sauce and a side of beets and cucumbers, filet of salmon with rice and string beans, grilled chicken with bell peppers and asparagus, fried calamari with sweet marinara sauce. My favorite was the turkey smothered with a sweet wine sauce and cucumbers sliced into thick pieces, always cold and refreshing. The salmon with a squeeze of lemon tasted juicy and tender. I enjoyed steamed asparagus dipped into mayonnaise. The steamed vegetables were always fresh. The calamari was fried and crunchy and left me craving more. The meals were healthy and delicious, a full gourmet experience.

It took me awhile to become accustomed to these new dinners. My host mom would talk about having to review her employees, while my host father served me spinach soup as if that was normal. Over the course of five months, I learned to eat vegetables and not snack between meals. I also learned to discuss the world with my host family over the meal. Back home, my parents would talk about the same problems—the misery of poverty and the insults of bosses. But their voices held no sense of entitlement or of political consciousness. Their faces showed an understanding of the harshness of daily life—and their dream that my sister and I would not suffer as they had.

For me, healthy food, smaller quantities, and higher prices are symbols of a middle-class lifestyle. Eating healthy is easier for those with money—and natural to them. Eating smaller portions but more variety is a luxury bestowed upon those who are certain of another meal. Fatty foods—homemade or processed—and lower prices are the trademarks of the working class. Minimum-wage jobs and lack of child care make it harder for parents to find the time and energy to think about and prepare healthy food alternatives.

As a descendant of farmers and blue-collar workers who still live from paycheck to paycheck, I now have a college degree, good meals behind me, and a precarious new sense of entitlement. I didn't grow up like my white college friends or the Chilean couple talking about sixteenth-century Roman invasions over turkey. My family and I saw twentieth-century American invasions into Latin America on the Spanish news while we ate plate after plate of *arroz con frijoles*. We wondered if it was *"el fin del mundo"*—the end of the world. We ate real food—cheap, easy to make, fast—always with the awareness that the world could make meals harder for us to have.

I am left wondering what types of dinners and talks I will have with my own future family. It is hard to be at home everywhere. I was never fully comfortable in Chile or at college, though I've come to enjoy eating to jazz music and sipping wine with dinner. I try to understand my parents' reality, but every day it just seems farther away. I'll never feel their hardships, and my children will not understand where the wrinkles under their grandparents' eyes came from. I hope my children will feel at home at any dinner table, but I know they will grow accustomed to eating like my Chilean host family. I probably will not make fried squid, but I will make a pretty tasty rice with black beans dish. Our conversations about Third World politics will carry the privilege of taking future meals for granted. My kids will probably live in a suburban house with nice furniture, and I do not know if there will be meat at every meal, but I hope to give them dinners with friends and family—more instead of less, and plenty of laughter. They will learn that dinner is not always a dining "experience," but that there is always a lot to be thankful for.

IT'S JUST BLOOD

Hadassah M. Hill

I sell my drugged-up blood for rent money, been doing it for about a year now. It's not so bad, either. Just a few days of lockdown, and then you walk away with a small stack of bills. Pay the rent, kids: That's the first priority. Then you can drink for a few days. Take out your best girl, go to the by-the-pound thrift store, buy eggs and bread, give the phone company the crumbs.

Listen. At twenty-two, I found myself in Canada, with a newly minted degree in the liberal arts and a newly emptied bank account. Genius is what they called me in school, and that's exactly the opposite of what it was to decide to stay in the amazing foreign country without money, access to money, or papers that would allow me to get a job and make some money. I was living in Toronto—New York City minus the crime and sex harassment, plus Commonwealth quirkiness, fabulous queer artists everywhere, and an economy that allowed me to have an apartment for the price of a leaky closet anywhere else.

On top of it all, there was a girl. No, there was The Girl. Stay here, I thought to myself. Pull something off. Having started out as a bookworm charity-case kid, I was about to try to scam survival. Having had to scrounge before, I figured I could do it again.

So I signed a lease and proceeded to look for work. That didn't go so good, and even the sweet deals soured when I was told, "And we would need a visa for you to work for us." Cash jobs are scarce, found almost zip zero for myself, and they're so sketchy anyway. The best I got was a quick job working for "Nate," putting concrete on asbestos-filled walls for nine dollars an hour, cash. But Nate was an alcoholic, didn't start work before 2 P.M., never kept at it after 6:00, and didn't want to see my face more than three times a week. Fine for temporary beer money, not so good for self-support.

I tried working at a vintage store, but my boss was a skeezy dude who never let me have a break from reorganizing stinky jeans, and he touched me too much. I quit by calling in and saying, "I'm not coming into work today . . . or ever again." The dread of it had made me nauseous. I considered turning tricks, but the fear of the backs of cop cars and deportment orders haunted me after each interview I did with an agency. I never went to any of the calls I got. The worry and the risk were too much. I was trying to stay in Canada, not get myself kicked out.

Looking without much hope in the paper one day, I saw an ad in the back—after the apartments, before the massage girls. "Are you between 18–50 years of age and in good heath? Available between June 12–14 and 19–21 inclusive? Call us to register for a medical examination; qualifying subjects will receive $1,025 upon study completion." Now I don't know about you, but that seemed like the riches of Madonna to me. So I called, and answered their questions: name, age, address, health history. It was all going fine until the nice interviewing lady said, "Are you a smoker?" I proudly answered, "Yes," and the nice lady said, "Sorry, but we can't use you," and ended the conversation. I sat alone in my apartment cursing my cigarettes, and then smoked one to ease the pain.

Next day I called a different place and had the sense to tell them I was not a smoker. I was recruited for a preliminary medical examination. I quit smoking for a day or two before going in for the exam, and it was a good thing too, because they did a test on my piss to make sure. They weighed, measured, and charted my body to determine my usefulness for their scientific experiment. I got a whack of paperwork detailing the test they wanted me to participate in, for a nasal decongestant that had already been tested on some other people. They told me to call back in a few days to find out if I had been accepted.

After finding out I was in, I was given the rundown: show up between 5:30 and 8 P.M. on the appointed day, consume no caffeine, alcohol, or grapefruit juice for forty-eight hours prior, bring your toiletries and a book or magazine. "You'll be here for a while, and you'll get bored," the woman on the phone said. Overnight for two nights? Away from my bike and my shoes and my lovers and my Internet? "Bored" sounded like the nicest way to say it.

My girlfriend and all my friends were terrified for me. "You're going to take a weird drug and then what?" they said. I said, "They're going to take samples of my blood every half hour for a few hours, then every hour for awhile, then a few times more, and then I get to go home. That's it." Everyone was real concerned. Where was I going to be? Could I leave? Was I safe? Would I be O.K.? I was concerned about all these things, too, but I didn't want to freak everyone out even more. The Girl made me a card to keep close to my heart when I went, a guinea pig cut out of pink construction paper. It listed all the dirty things she would do to me upon my safe arrival back in her arms.

So, here's what happened. I showed up, checked in, was relieved of my bladder's contents, and brought to the storage room, where I left my shoes and clothes and donned the oversized lavender scrubs they gave me. After I was let in to a heavily locked room, a guard searched my bag to make sure I had no candy or herbal toothpaste, and I sat down at a plastic table. There were a dozen or so other people in the room, all in the same scrubs as me, looking either semi-dazed or oddly comfortable. There were lots of couches and chairs, and in the center of the room was a massive TV. On the periphery were smaller rooms with sliding-glass doors and bunk beds, our sleeping quarters. There was a small reading room in the back, where you could close the door and sit quietly. I sat in there for a while, trying to figure out if this was like being in jail or not. I had a carefully measured snack, and then the TV went on and I watched in wonder as everyone remained silently glued to it for the rest of the evening, until lights out was called and we climbed into our assigned bunk beds to sleep.

We were woken up at 6 A.M. the next day for breakfast, which we had to eat beginning at a certain minute, and finish within a prescribed amount of time. This was to ensure that what was in our bodies was completely regulated, I guess. My eggs were cold and my toast soggy, but I ate it so as to not be a whiner. Everybody hates a whiner, and since these people were about to start poking me with needles for the next twenty-two hours, it seemed wise to get on their good side.

The strangest part of doing a drug study is not the eighteen hours of consecutive Hollywood movies available for viewing each day, or the fact that you're giving blood at minutely regulated intervals, or how most of the people doing it with you know each other, or even that you can't go outside, or to the bathroom without telling someone. No, the weirdest part of selling blood is the moment of dosing. This is when you take the medication that this whole thing is about in the first place. This is the only time the TV actually gets turned off. Everyone has to listen close for their "subject number" to be called, though you're sitting in a lineup anyway, so it would be hard to miss your turn. Then you go to a counter, where three or four people in lab coats are watching you. Someone tells you not to chew, to drink all your water, not to touch the pill, and to go . . . exactly . . . now! Then someone checks your mouth with a flashlight to make sure you aren't chipmunking the medicine.

From then on, it's pretty straightforward. I had a chart, and at the times on my chart I went to the "Bleeding Room" where someone took my blood. Sometimes I had to get my blood pressure checked or have an ECG. The rest of the time I could do things like talk on the phone, lie around, read a book; anything nonstrenuous. I brought some embroidery, and found it very fulfilling to be covering a skirt in tiny sperms while horrible Mel Gibson seduced underweight women on a screen somewhere in the background.

I had to sleep there one more night, and after a final blood draw in the morning, I was released back into the world. I got to the bus stop and smoked a cigarette, feeling woozy and victorious for surviving. The fun part is getting drunk off one beer later in the day, because you lost so much blood—although it's less than if you had donated to the Red Cross.

The not-so-fun part is doing it again the next week, because most of these studies are in two parts: one for an "approved" drug, the other for the trial drug. But at the end, I'm done with my book or my sewing project, I've caught up with all my friends on the phone, and I have money power, which takes me where I gotta go.

The studies don't seem to be affecting me negatively—I don't have a third eye or hair loss, just a tiny scar in the crook of my right arm, where my good vein is. The drugs I take are generally really normal prescription types, like antibiotics or antihistamines. I won't do studies on depression drugs because brain chemistry is so touchy, but the body, especially when young, is an amazing processing center, filtering out poison like it's going out of style. Think about how shitty alcohol is for you. If you drink, your body is much more assaulted by that. Taking one pill doesn't seem so dangerous.

When I was a kid and thought about my future, I often had visions of scuzzy bars and sweaty cash transfers. Or I thought I would work at Starbucks forever with all the other college graduates, or just scam through life until I became famous. When those scenarios don't work, when your family is more broke than you and you want to keep going because you've found a community, found love, found the best apartment, when you need to save money to emigrate and find a way to live somewhere and completely avoid cops, well, big chunks of cash in exchange for a few days' time and some easily replaceable plasma sounds about as good as it's gonna get.

My mom finds it appalling that I do this. She says she prays for me the whole time I'm in the lab. My friends find it either vaguely pitiful or amazing, depending on how broke they are. I find it a way to survive. And after all, how often do you meet a chick who works four days a month and can still afford to take you out? I'm just waiting for the word to get out, so I can meet a gal on the inside and fuck her when the staff isn't looking.

GHETTO FABULOUS

Tina Fakhrid-Deen

Buying a house in the 'hood was a sociopolitical decision for me and my husband. I didn't want us to be the type of Black folks who get a little money and flee to the suburbs, away from our people. I live in Chicago. I was born on the west side of one of the most segregated cities in the nation, in the Jane Addams projects, a place commonly referred to as "the ghetto." It was a few miles west of downtown and close to everything imaginable—a prime location.

My family was poor, but resilient. We were no strangers to food stamps, roaches, and hallways that smelled of urine. We often had to eat those black-and-white-labeled generic brands and drink powdered milk, which I despised. I learned early on that sugar on a slice of bread or mixed with a glass of water made a tasty afternoon snack when peanut butter and jelly or Kool-Aid were unavailable.

I am proud of my roots and my complex identity, so it makes me sick when I hear people speak negatively about the ghetto, the place that I called home for many years. It is common to hear white and Black middle-class teens, in a skewed attempt to embrace hip-hop culture, say offensive things like, "Oh, my God, he is acting so ghetto," or, "Look at my big ghetto booty." Although the word "ghetto" refers to a section of the city densely populated by a certain minority group and was formerly where all Jewish people were dumped in some Eastern European countries (and later in Chicago and other big, American cities as well), the term is used quite differently now.

To those on the outside looking in, the term "ghetto" is now synonymous with being Black, dirty, attitudinal, ignorant, lazy, uneducated, and dangerous; it has taken on the same connotations that the term "nigger" historically has had. However different, they are both politically loaded terms used to denigrate poor Blacks, but to acknowledge that would be politically incorrect. "Ghetto" is the new code word for "low-income Black person." Whites won't acknowledge it because it feels too close to being racist, and middle-class Blacks won't acknowledge it because in their hearts, they know that using the word is a sad attempt to distance themselves from the lower class, to assimilate and be accepted by mainstream culture. It would be a public admission that poor Blacks are reduced to frightening caricatures, misunderstood by the majority of American society, still overtly oppressed.

I am ghetto. I love hip-hop, Ice Cube, and the Geto Boys. I have a big butt and snap my neck back and forth when I'm cussing someone out. I look good in cornrows and wild afros. I can do the "booty" dances with the best of them and I still say "ain't" to get my point across. I also have good parents, who always encouraged me to be the best and to speak my mind. As a result, I have a master's degree in education. No, my mama is not on welfare and yes, my father was present while I was growing up. I've never committed a crime, unless you count the time I stole a piece of bubble gum from 7-Eleven and returned it two minutes later out of guilt. I have a beautiful husband, not a "baby daddy." I've traveled to at least six different countries, studied abroad, and wear "ethnic" thrift-store dresses to work. I plan to teach our child Spanish and sign language. My ghetto identity is more than the latest booty-shake video, it is my foundation, and it reverberates through every facet of me—textured and rich. And no, I am not the exception.

My old neighborhood was ghetto. The scent of month-old chicken grease filled most homes, and stained blinds hung in the place of flowery curtains. There were scattered winos on the sidewalks, glass shards on the playground instead of wood chips, rampant petty crime, graffiti on the walls, and boarded-up windows on some apartments. There were also community centers where we could go and play board games and get juice and a "choke" sandwich (so damn dry you could choke eating them) until our parents got home. Hard-working parents worked several jobs to make ends meet and to provide a good, loving home for their families.

In school, we had spelling bees and learned Spanish in kindergarten. Caring adults with knowing eyes watched over us if our parents weren't around. We all knew each other's names and who to call when a child got out of line in the street. We were a community. My friends were ghetto. We did ghetto things, like drinking buttermilk with cookies and mixing Kool-Aid with sugar, giggling at the sour-sweet taste in our red-stained mouths. We played double dutch with a long extension cord while singing "take a peach, take a plum." Each time the jump rope hit one of us in the face, we had bitter fistfights, wind-milling with our eyes closed, hoping to make contact. At Halloween, we got yelled at or whipped for throwing eggs, not because it was childish and rude, but because we were screwing with the food supply. Some of us grew up to be construction workers, accountants, and teachers, while others became gang affiliates, hood rats, and drug dealers. Some moved out of the projects; some remain to this day. Some went off to college; others went off to prison. Regardless, we all shared the same history, cried the same tears, and mirrored the same struggle—withstanding poverty.

My family moved away from the projects when I was about six. We lived in the suburbs and then down South for a brief stint, but moved back to an urban area on the North Side of Chicago marked by many of the same characteristics as my former ghetto. Basically, we were still poor and struggling to survive. Upon returning to Chicago from college, I searched the city for housing. I drove back to my old neighborhood and, to my chagrin, found most of it had been torn down—shiny new town homes with skater boys stood in its place. It was now called "University Village," because a local university had bought up most of the property. Even the hospital where many of my friends and I were born had disappeared without a trace. It was almost as if we had never existed. It made my blood boil that all of those poor people had been displaced, and I wondered where they had gone. I blamed middle-class America and greedy developers. I accused the mayor and his cronies of turning a blind eye to what was happening in poor communities like mine.

I wanted to live in a place where all socioeconomic backgrounds were represented, no one above the other. I finally decided to move back to the North Side, for the diversity in ethnicities, cultures, and economic status. The local fruit market sold everything from *kimchi* and plantains to yucca and collard greens. *Elote* carts rolled down the street with hot ears of corn as often as ice cream trucks. Blue-collar and white-collar workers rode the el train together each morning. There were little coffee shops on several corners, adorned near the entrances by the occasional evening prostitute or homeless man. In my building lived a Jamaican drug dealer who often threw wild parties with the scent of cheeba oozing under the door; an alcoholic white man and his six-foot grocery cart–toting girlfriend, who fought like Ali and Frazier in a title bout; a spiritual Black vegetarian who swore that a cat's purr meant that it was going to attack her; a wiry ballerina who rented out her place every other month; some Eastern Europeans who spoke little English and managed the building; me and my mathematician husband; and an interracial couple who just seemed shady.

Slowly, many of the buildings in our area were converted to condos, the asking prices beyond ridiculous. The poor were being forced to move out, just like in my old neighborhood. They left a few Section Eight homes intact, for nostalgia's sake. Although gentrification came rapidly to our neighborhood, we weren't directly impacted until my mother (who lived down the street from us) was forced to move out of her tiny one-bedroom apartment when her rent jumped from $475 to $1,250 a month. Then our building changed hands, and the new owner threatened to almost double the rent for our modest one-bedroom. We all needed to move, and fast. My mother purchased her first home on the far South Side. Loving the diversity of the North Side, my husband and I tried to find another local property to purchase, but the price hikes were happening everywhere. We considered the suburbs, but quickly came back to reality. Why buy into the reverse white flight and allow upper-class whites to move back into the comforts and convenience of the city while we got stuck out in the boon-docks, disconnected from everything we knew? So we did the most intelligent thing we could think of, we invested in Bronzeville, a historic South Side community.

During the great migration of the early 1900s, many Blacks emigrated from the South in hopes of landing industrial jobs in Chicago. Bronzeville was one of the only areas of the city that southern Blacks were allowed to live in. It is legendary for its sizzling-hot blues scene and notorious 47th St., a strip of juke joints, jazz cafes, restaurants, and hotels. This is where famous Black artists such as Billie Holiday and Ella Fitzgerald came to perform and stay when they had a gig in town. For years after its heyday, Bronzeville had been a poverty-stricken area filled with crime, despair, and little development. This was now one of the hot spots in the city to move to, because of its accessibility to downtown and the lakefront, and its affordable housing.

In a matter of days, we found a beautiful three-bedroom condo with a monthly mortgage in the same price bracket as our old apartment's rent increase. Set right on the main boulevard—named after a well-known Black civil rights leader—we could see all types of Black people walking up and down the street. This was the first time that I had been back in an all-Black area since my days in the ghetto and the South. It was exciting and wonderful, although I did miss the ethnic diversity of the North Side. There was a new Black-owned poetry cafe and a bank, and the alder-woman's office was less than a block away. It was rumored that a comedy club, performing arts theater, art gallery, and bookstore were in develop-ment on the next corner. Across the street, a sign boasted a new town-home development starting at $350,000. My husband and I thought that our neighbors were fabulous and incredibly nice. We had two lesbian pastors across the hall, three outgoing drug dealers, otherwise known as "pharmaceutical representatives," two PhD's, an ex-cop, a lawyer, and several high-powered businesswomen. We were all so close that it was like living in the dorms again.

I soon realized that I had somehow crossed over and was officially middle class. It was confusing, because I wasn't like the bourgeois Blacks who knew nothing about hard times and mocked the accursed lot of poor folks. I was different. I cared about civil rights for everyone. I didn't turn my nose up at the thought of eating pig feet or chitlins. I didn't fear that my property value would go down because poor folks lived next door. And I didn't refer to all less fortunate people, especially the expressive or thuggish-looking ones, as "ghetto." Then my whole reality changed. Within a week of our moving in to our new building there were two attempted robberies. I was four months pregnant and actually heard them kicking in my neighbor's door. A few weeks later, someone's car was broken into; then more robbery attempts in the coming months. I began to fear coming home late in the evening. As a pregnant woman in her third trimester, I was truly defenseless. My mind began betraying me. I questioned whether this neighborhood was good enough—safe enough—for me and my family. I feared the possibility of my child picking up broken crack vials in the neighborhood park during our afternoon strolls. I thought about sending our daughter to the substandard neighborhood schools. I thought about someone actually getting into our home, violating us and everything we've worked so hard for. I thought about moving—moving far away from crime, far away from my present reality, and even farther away from the ghetto we now lived in. It no longer felt like home—it felt like prison. It felt dangerous. It felt unforgiving. I felt like I was being punished for leaving the 'hood and coming back with a pot to piss in. I saw jealous eyes ogle me as I entered our six-foot gate, making sure it slammed behind me. I became resentful, fighting rage. I felt like a traitor.

I had become that middle-class asshole who moves in and pushes aside the poor residents, who are rightfully angry. They wanted the good life too. They wanted big-screen TVs and Jacuzzis like us. They wanted to feel important and respected, as we did. They also craved quality community resources for their families. No matter how I tried to frame it, I had become one of the powerful pawns in this gentrification game, with the poorest of Bronzeville being knocked clear off the board. Like magic, with our middle-class presence, the schools would begin to get better, more commercial development would find its way to the area, and politicians and policemen would make special visits to our condo association meetings to hear our concerns. We would complain about the crime and beg for the removal of it, of "them." My sensitivity for the wretched poor would wear thin. Ill feelings would grow between us and "them" until someone gave in and moved on. There could be no coexistence between the classes. We misunderstood and distrusted each other too much. There could be no community here.

Not until we stop to realize that we're all in this together. Not until I use my newfound middle-class power to advocate for the right to decent and affordable living for my new neighbors, here in Bronzeville. Not until I help them to advocate for themselves. Not until I realize that some of these residents don't want or need our middle-class handouts because they were doing just fine before we got here. Not until I understand that many of these families are just like mine was back in the day, working hard and trying to keep food on the table. Not until I treat them as equals. Not until I stop being scared and open my mouth to say "hello" to the skeptical faces that eye me daily. Not until I recognize that the ones trying to rob us are just lost souls with no hope or heart left (that doesn't mean I won't keep calling the cops). Not until I get the resentment out of my heart.

The ghetto is a community filled with ups and downs, struggles and survivors and people sticking around hoping that things will get better. Being ghetto is so much more than a new catchphrase or a hip-hop song; it's an identity, a reflection of our economy, and a way of life. Just as hip-hop will be in my blood and spirit forever, so will the ghetto. I will transcend the box that us ghetto folks have been put into and create a new space. I will make people think before using the term "ghetto" to refer to any person, place, or thing. I will fight for the right to be ghetto, even when my back's against the wall, being violated by those I'm trying to stand up for. That's keeping it real—real ghetto. As a people, when one of us suffers, we all suffer. In my heart, I know that we ain't a true community until we take an honest look at each other and begin to embrace every part of our intricately woven culture. Black folks must get a handle on the crabs-in-a-barrel syndrome, and learn to stand strong, together.

GETTING OUT

Frances Varian

Fear tastes like metal on the back of my tongue. It sits heavy on my rib cage, making it difficult to breathe. A thousand small pinches beneath my skin. One hundred bells ringing in my skull at the same time. Fear is my sun and I orbit around it.

And everyone I was born to orbits in the solar system of the punch-clock. There was never a time when my face wasn't turned toward something greater than myself. Fear and poverty breed shame. Exhaustion and disappointment make everything taste bitter. The tired body cannot convince the racing mind to sleep. The sun will rise. Then we will work. These are things you know instinctively. Without money bad things will happen to you and you won't be able to stop them. The only way to get money is to work for it and there are only two kinds of work: smart or hard. You enter the world, pull for air, and wait for payday.

I don't want to write about class. To write about class is to pull a carefully placed bandage from a wound and poke at it. What are my choices? I can romance you with stories of working-class pride and sacrifice. I can tug at your heartstrings with tales of desperation and injustice. I can show you my scars. I can try to describe the rage. I can tell you what it feels like to be the daughter of a janitor. I can tell you what it feels like to be a graduate of Vassar College. I can tell you how to simulate a blowjob over the phone for strangers. But after I am done telling you all of these necessary things I still won't have any money. And I will still be afraid. So what are my choices?

Here's how my Roman Catholic Polish family likes to play a game I call Wheel of Getting the Fuck Out of Here. It's a game that most working-class people play on some level. First, everyone has a really screwed-up childhood with abusive, alcoholic parents. Then everyone finds their own partners and makes babies. (In the Polish Catholic version, the babies must come after a proper Catholic wedding.) The most important thing to know about Wheel of Getting the Fuck Out of Here is that you, the Player, will never get the fuck out of here. The only one who can possibly get out is that baby you just made. Your job is to move the Game Piece (baby) around the board so that she is able to "work smart." If she works smart, she will make money. When she has money, she will not be so afraid. In order to move the Game Piece you must work so hard you cannot remember your middle name. You must spin the wheel to see if your dead dreams can be reincarnated in your child. And most important, you must teach your baby the importance of getting out. You must hold yourself up to her time and time again as inspiration to flee.

I am a wayward Game Piece, maybe a design flaw. In this particular game the Players (my parents) did most everything correctly. They worked and sacrificed and buried their dreams. They did everything they possibly could to make sure they won this game. They had no idea that the object of their struggles would grow up to reject it just as she was on the verge of getting the fuck out. If they craved a life easier lived, they would not experience it through me.

When I was still a child, we drove past the most spectacular group of buildings near our home in upstate New York. It was Vassar College. My parents said it was a school for rich girls. They said Jackie Kennedy went to Vassar. I thought it looked mysterious and beautiful, like castles. (I would later learn the term Gothic as it applies to architecture and black lipstick.) I wanted to be there so much I could taste it above the fear and I said, "I'm going to Vassar just like Jackie Kennedy."

And that's kind of what I did: I went to Vassar. I just did it a little differently than the former First Lady. Upon hearing my childish declaration, my father quit one of his two full-time jobs and obtained a position at the college as a security guard. He had learned that if he was an employee of the college his child's tuition would be waived, providing his kid could get accepted. I was not yet in middle school.

My father was born in 1927. I was not born until he was forty-nine years old and he has no other children. He is a charming man. Handsomely rugged in appearance and quiet, he is almost immediately likeable. He's towed cars, been a courier, a school-bus driver, a janitor, a security guard, and many other miscellaneous things. He has worked at least two full-time jobs, more than eighty hours every week, for at least forty years. He was gone often when I was growing up and was frequently exhausted when he came back home. My dad's work meant he was on his feet, cleaning, lifting, moving, and protecting, almost all the time. He is still, at seventy-six years old, part of the invisible fleet of people who keep our bathrooms clean and our mountain bikes from being stolen. Kept invisible because who among us wants to look at the stranger cleaning our shit off of public toilets? His is a life dedicated to the service of thousands who will never know his name.

My father adores me. I often suspect it was the combination of his enormous strength and endurance and his devotion to the women in his life that led me to love butches and trannybois as an adult. It was for me he played Wheel of Getting the Fuck Out of Here like no one had ever played before. This is the romance I warned you about.

I would come to learn, as a student, that tuition remission was considered a perk for professors and their families. It was not unusual for the child of a faculty member to apply to Vassar. But in 1994, the kids of security guards came knocking only slightly more frequently than they had in Jackie Kennedy's day. It left me with an out-of-place feeling that wasn't necessarily unpleasant but that has remained with me ever since.

None of that mattered when I entered Vassar. The castles, the ghosts, all of the people with nothing better to do than take their brains out on long walks enchanted me. We were doing work. It wasn't lazy to sit around all day and read—it was mandatory. I took whatever crumbling faith I had remaining in the Catholic Church and placed my bet on humanism. I was going to become a scholar committed to the pursuit of knowledge and I was going to work smart. Vassar was powerful enough to catapult me so far Out I would never have to look back again. My first week of school, dozens of kids stomped around complaining because they hadn't gotten accepted into Brown. I had no idea what "Brown" was.

This experience, I imagine, is similar to that of other working-class kids who are the first in their family to go to college, or a certain type of college. My entire life thus far had been a battle strategy to get me to this place. Everyone's resources were used in this endeavor and now I was on my own to navigate the Seven Sisters experience. The rules, language, and vantage point of the upper class are different from mine. They know very little about the lives of working-class and poor people. I watched professors from one of the most liberal colleges in the United States walk past my father like he was a polite ghost. Perhaps we are only interesting in theory.

Throughout my freshman year, the majority of my friends on campus were cleaning ladies, security guards, and cafeteria workers. They were the army who made it possible for me to study feminist film theory, *Othello*, and the elements of moral philosophy. I was, unequivocally, the safest person on campus. My bathroom was the cleanest. My meals were often free. I was their collective darling. They were watching someone on the verge of getting out and they guarded me as something precious.

I loved school. I loved spending entire Sundays in the enormous stone library with its secret passages, stained glass, and ghosts. I knew the information I had at hand was powerful because it was so well hidden. The library was for members of the Vassar community only. And of that community, only faculty and students made use of the resource. Staff cleaned and guarded the building, but they did not check out books very often.

The better I understood my education, the angrier I became that most working-class and poor people are denied one. Why are the children of doctors, lawyers, and engineers taught the mysteries of existence while the children of janitors and waitresses are taught fear? I developed a preoccupation with my own inadequacies, aided by a few professors of elitism. To combat my growing anxiety, I began to envision myself a class spy. I would soak up all of the information they could give me and run reconnaissance for my team.

With time I began to question the validity of Wheel of Getting the Fuck Out of Here, which felt very much like questioning the existence of the sun. If I was so close to getting out, why was I still afraid? Why did I want to leave the people who had been so good to me? The reality of my upper-class peers was so drastically different from my own—did I really want to become exactly like them? And even if I wanted to, I knew it would be impossible. I could make millions of dollars and I would still wake up every morning searching for something greater than myself. I could transform myself into the most sophisticated intellect and they would still be able to smell my fear.

There exist the wealthy and the working class. At Vassar I learned the two are not mutually exclusive. No matter how rich I might become, I will always be the daughter of a janitor. I will always look the woman who empties my garbage in the face. I will always say thank you to the man who serves me lunch. I am one of them, and I do not want to Get Out unless they can come too.

That was it for me, the Game Piece. I would not take a lucrative corporate job and I would not participate in the brain drain of the working class. Game Over. The culture of the people I come from is as valuable as any I have studied. Our language, our unique perspectives, our strengths and weaknesses deserve critical attention. It is not our status as workers that prevents our happiness, but the glaring and obscene disparity between our paychecks and the paychecks of the ruling class. Working-class culture is not something we should run from even if we are offered the opportunity to escape poverty.

Poverty is not a natural conclusion. It is an invention. We are not poor because we are inferior as a group of people; we are poor because it is imperative to the global economy that a limitless supply of labor exist. The labor must be cheap and disposable.

This Game Piece respectfully declines the opportunity to exploit the labor of somebody else's mother or father. As long as we believe it is desirable to get out of the working class, we will continue to be afraid. Assimilation does not free us; it whitewashes the most obvious lie ever told. The Game is a con. The Wheel is fixed. It's time to invent a new one.

What are our choices?

MY MOTHER
WAS A WHORE

Nikki Levine

It's something I've known for much of my life, though I couldn't even begin to say it out loud until I sucked my first dick for money. It's never been a big conversation piece, not something I bring up to people, because it always seemed like any other job to me. Not a lot of people actually had jobs in Jersey City when I was growing up, at least not legal ones, and definitely none of the people around me. I didn't have a home for years, unless you count other people's cars, motel-room floors, and pitched tents in Lincoln Park behind the projects we were kicked out of after a drug bust occurred in our tiny apartment.

"We were dealt a shitty hand," my grandma once told me after I interrupted her watching *Wheel of Fortune*, her weekday 7:30 scream-along session, to complain about what the kids around town had been making fun of me for that day (I'd worn the same shirt two days in a row). "SOLVE THE PUZZLE, YOU FUCKIN' SCHMUCK!" she'd be yelling at the polished people on the black-and-white screen who'd stare blankly at obvious phrases, or at least phrases that were obvious to Grandma. As the oldest and the first-generation American, as well as the loudest in the family, Grandma was regarded by everyone as the genius, the one who knew everything. It still blows my mind that she never figured out my mother was a whore—or maybe she was so smart that she knew the whole time but kept her knowledge a secret from my mother and me.

Grandma kicked us out of the family's average-sized Ocean County house in 1986. We had lived there for almost a year, along with my aunt, her husband, Grandma, Grandpa, and Grandma's parents. I was in first grade, and all I knew is we were "moving to the city." Mom had met a guy named Tony, who I hated from the start because of his creepy voice and the fact that he wore ribbed tank tops over thermal underwear shirts in the summertime. He wore a gold chain with someone's head hanging from it like a museum exhibit. I later learned this was Jesus, someone that the Catholics worshipped. I knew nothing about that in my sheltered Reform-Jew world. Reform, mostly because we couldn't afford to join a temple. Grandma said we had to leave because she didn't want my mother to be with Tony—who I later found out wore those thermal shirts to hide the track marks that stained his arm like paint on a canvas. "MY WAY OR THE HIGHWAY!" Grandma screamed at my mother one day as she opened the broken front door, pointing to the proverbial "highway." My mother chose the highway, a.k.a. drugs and the chance to be a Mafia wife, and we moved to Jersey City.

My mother walked the streets for years in her late twenties and early thirties. She was a genius and could have been the doctor that her grandma always told her she'd better be. But by the time she was twenty-eight, it wasn't an option for her. My mother was a heroin addict. Her addiction was like having another child to keep alive with the easy money she made with her body, with her hands, her mouth, her pussy.

My mother became a whore because she had a daughter and a deadbeat ex-husband. She was a single mother in a dead, brick city in northern New Jersey, dividing her time between finding places for me to sleep and having sex with strangers. Tony was living with his parents, who hated my mother because she wasn't Italian. Regardless, we were allowed to eat Sunday dinner at their house. Tony slept in their garage and always had needles hanging out of his arm when we'd show up. He said he loved me and wanted me to call him "Daddy."

My mother's addiction was serious, it controlled almost everything, but she never forgot that she had a daughter to take care of. She'd cry us both to sleep at night on motel-room floors, the floors of her johns who were kind enough to let their homeless whore and her daughter sleep in their $20-per-night first-floor unit. They'd wake up early in the morning and shoo us out in time for me to get to school. My mother would walk me to school in her stiletto heels and black cat suit. The other kids thought she was a goddess just like I did. We didn't know she was a whore, or that a whore could be a goddess.

My mother was a whore. The black sheep of the family. Divorced from my father and now dating Italian men exclusively. She wanted to be Italian, not Jewish. My mother dated Mafia bottom-feeders and changed my last name in my school registration so I wouldn't have to be a "Levine" anymore. I was now an Italian girl, a DiFeo, just like her and her Tony. I was sworn to secrecy.

She sold cocaine on the job. She didn't have a real pimp, just Tony, who she was selling cocaine for—to make money to support his habit. I knew she was out in the streets for me, though, her daughter that she didn't mean to have but loved more than anything in the world. She was a dealer, but the money she made from whoring was different from the drug money. When I was thirteen or fourteen she told me the story of what she was really doing. How she never spent drug money on me, that's what the fuck money was for. My dad disappeared and didn't pay child support; she had to get money for me somehow.

My mother always told me that I should respect the sex industry, though not in those words. We were inner-city to the core; she didn't know that it was an "industry." I look at all of the hype about sex work now, how it's the new cool feminist occupation and how young whores are spreading the gospel of prostitution to the Third Wave, the no wave, the whatever-the-fuck wave of feminists now. Unfortunately, most of this is on the Internet or in fanzines. In most cases, inner-city whores and their children do not have access to this kind of information. I've come across a multitude of fanzines and Internet websites geared toward The Sex Worker—resources that are intended to provide safety tips to, and instill the feeling of community among, sex workers. My mother was an older woman (relatively) from the streets of Jersey City; if someone had handed her a modern fanzine about sex work, she most likely wouldn't have understood what was presented to her. Phrases like "sex work" would have been alien to her. A loner in the industry, my mother would have shunned the idea of a "safety call"; she was too proud to have anyone else know what she was doing when she left our roach-infested apartment in her cat suit and cheap, broken stilettos. Though I think it's important that sex-worker harm-reduction information be brought into the inner cities for people like my mother, I'm unsure as to who would be capable of translating information originally intended for college-oriented young people into something that an older inner-city prostitute with not much formal education could process.

Before she was a whore, my mother was a stripper. I would try on her costumes when she wasn't looking; they always made me feel so glamorous. I'd use duct tape to keep the thongs up high on my little thighs; pasties covered my tiny five-year-old tits. I'd dance around our tiny bedroom to her collection of 45s, singing along in my shrill baby voice while slowly removing my sequined panties. "*I wanna rock with you . . .*" I'd sing along with Michael Jackson. When Mom would catch me, she'd move the needle off the record and tell me it was O.K. to wear the outfits, but not O.K. to remove them while dancing. She told me that she never got fully unclothed for any job. She said she hoped I would never have to do what she does.

After a year of fruitless efforts to find a way to escape Tony (who had been beating both of us and taking my mother's money), she finally called the police on him. I'll never forget that day—I sat on the counter of the apartment we were sharing with another family for the month and watched Tony as he carefully loaded his syringe and got down to business and suddenly the front door was broken down and in pieces on the floor. Police filled the room, my mother grabbed me, and we hid in the corner behind an undercover agent who we had been getting to know. Her name was Michelle and she helped my mother set the trap. We were free.

We entered the world of the mysterious witness-protection program. We were put up in a hotel on Staten Island and told to wait. We waited, and during this time my mother detoxed. I had no idea what was wrong with her. While she lay in bed curled into the fetal position, screaming about the demons she saw, I would roam the streets of Staten Island looking for a cure. I described my mother's symptoms to random street runners, dealers, thugs, whores, you name it. Finally, I met a guy named Gooch who told me he had what my mother needed. He handed me a clear bag with whitish brown powder in it. A heart decorated the bag. I brought it home to my mother, excited that I had the antidote to her sickness. She looked at the bag and threw up, commanding me to flush it down the toilet quickly. She told me that bag contained the demon. I did as she told me and lay next to her in the bed she'd soaked with her sweat, and she held me tight and told me she'd never be this sick again.

About a week later, my mother was feeling a lot better. We watched *Good Day New York* every morning, and my mother told me that if I saw myself on the show I shouldn't be scared, because we were moving. She didn't know where, but she said we'd have new names, new hairstyles, and new stories to tell people. Stories we'd need to maintain in order to keep us from Tony. Right as *Good Day New York* was ending and *I Love Lucy's* beginning credits rolled, the hotel phone rang. It was Michelle. She said we were not allowed to be a part of the program because my mother's drug test came out positive. At least, that's what my mom told me. The next day, we checked out of the hotel and moved to the shore for A Better Life, with the fear of Tony's return constantly lingering in the backs of our minds.

My mother became an agent at a "fantasy entertainment" company run by an old family friend named Lee. She was essentially a pimp—finding dancers for private parties and making sure she got Lee's cut. She made $5 an hour, which wasn't enough to pay for my lunch at school. It paid the rent, though, keeping us alive in our one-bedroom apartment in Brick, New Jersey. And it was off the books, so my mother was now able to collect welfare and get food stamps. The food stamps were embarrassing to me; I refused to go shopping with my mother when she used them. The town itself was mostly filled with families, "whole families," families with bay views and their own attics and basements that nobody lived in. Maybe they kept their toys there, or had a "family room." I don't even think there was a welfare office in town.

One day, Tony showed up on our doorstep, crying and begging to be let in. "I'm clean, I'm clean," he said over and over again. I wondered what his hygiene had to do with letting him into our tiny roach-infested apartment. He'd just get dirty again. And she let him in. He detoxed in my bedroom, and I wondered why they were both so sick all the time. Soon they were both feeling great. They had gone back to heroin, and Tony returned to dealing out of our apartment. I was once again to call him "Daddy," and I had to start walking differently. Apparently I didn't walk "heel-toe, heel-toe." This infuriated him, and he'd spend hours watching me walk around the house. On one particularly memorable occasion, he followed me around with a .357 Magnum and told me that I'd "better get it right." My mother screamed and cried, begging him not to hurt me. He used the gun to hit my mother in the face and she fell to the ground, bleeding and sobbing. I started to run to my mother but I also caught a pistol whip to the face and was knocked out immediately. I don't really remember what happened after that.

My mama was a whore but it didn't upset me. When money got tough after she died, I never thought of whoring. I figured I was too fat, too this, too that. I didn't want to be called a Whore. It seemed so dirty. But my mother taught me that if I needed to, I could be a whore and it wouldn't be terrible. It would be a job.

What am I now? My mother taught me how to take care of myself in the presence of older men. Older men were the ones who would fuck us over all the time. We were both deathly afraid of men in their forties. Mustaches, beards, white skin, little purple dicks. She taught me not to fear; she taught me how to take charge and make them fear me, which was a totally new concept. Mama taught me that if I had to be a whore, I wouldn't be scared or ashamed.

So when my hands clutch unfamiliar balls, my mouth on unfamiliar dicks, unfamiliar hands on my tits and grabbing for my pussy, I don't get frightened. My knife gives me power. My mother carried a gun. She also walked the streets, and did it alone. I work with my girlfriend and we do it sober, watching out for each other and keeping ourselves out of danger.

When they thrust green bills into my hands I remember my mother sucking dick for food stamps. I remember going hungry because there was a blizzard in Jersey City and she couldn't walk around in stilettos in the snow. Borrowing cranberry sauce from our next-door neighbors Dennis and Cathy, coke customers of Tony and my mom. They were adamant about us buying them another can once the sidewalks were plowed.

In 1999, AIDS claimed the life of my mother, thanks to Tony. She never shot anything into her veins—she snorted her dope. Tony, on the other hand . . .

My mother watches over me like an angel. It wasn't her time to go, but she did leave. She must have had a plan. She always had a plan.

I never thought I'd be here, a sex worker, a pro-domme, but I am and I'm not afraid. Because where I go, there's my mother, hovering to make sure I don't get hurt. And when their prying hands find their way to my pussy she intervenes, drawing everyone's attention to something across the street or across the room.

I walk into every call knowing my mother is there and that it's going to be O.K. I walk out of every call with a smile on my face because we're that much richer. I get my money, and I learned how from my mother, who was a genius, a goddess, and a whore.

FOR THOSE WHO LIKE TO DIG

Ricky Lee

At 4:15 A.M. the alarm goes off. I hit snooze . . . precious snooze. The girl had come in tossed at 3 A.M., wanting to get it on. I'd given her the keys to my place, which was maybe a mistake, but what can I say. Loneliness often leads to mistakes.

4:30—*son of a*—press snooze.

At 5 A.M., I shut off the alarm, sit up in bed, and listen closely by the window. Sounds like rain, a slow, persistent, San Francisco drizzle. Rain. I start making plans involving pay-per-view pornos, pizza, hot wings with a side of Ranch dressing—don't forget the Ranch—all stuff I can't afford, particularly because my check is gonna be short, but it's fucking Christmas, goddamn it, it's a *rain* day. I pull the curtain back slowly, very slowly, and stare out into the street below, where a small white Toyota pickup truck is doing laps around the block, no doubt lookin' for a hooker and a blowjob before work. The tires on the asphalt sound deceptively like a San Francisco rain shower.

I'm a laborer for a landscape construction company. My particular crew is working a large job up north, handling large tree plantings, sod, irrigation, and drainage. Some mornings I get a ride from my apartment. On these occasions I stand in front of my gate and watch the business of Capp

Street. Most of the girls working my street aren't so dressed up, and they're pretty strung out. Some of them are straight-up bulldaggers like me, workin' the streets in shorts and Converse sneakers. Sometimes the guys think I'm a hooker—the guy in the white truck propositioned me once. I told him I wasn't working, though in fact I was waiting for a ride to my shitty manual-labor job, same sort of work he was heading to, after he got off. Most days I gotta catch a train to get to a bus that gets me to a ride that will drive me an hour up north. All by 5 A.M.

I have already wasted so much time this morning, with my rain-day fantasy plans, that I can't shower. I step right into the jeans I stepped out of just a few hours earlier, and dirt pours out of the cuffs, making tiny pyramids on the floor. T-shirt, pleated flannel, ball cap, keys, cigarettes, wallet. The wallet is merely habit, as there is not much in it. I throw some French rolls and lunch meat in a plastic bag, plus two cups of ramen—one to eat, the other to barter with.

5:15. I hit Mission Street, beginning the sleepy, gender-dysphoric walk through my day. Rounding the corner, a tweaked-out hooker smiles flirtatiously in my direction, her smile drooping into annoyance as she realizes I'm a chick and she has just wasted her precious milliseconds. She flips her hair and quickly strides across the street. Crack dealers say, "What ya need girl?"

"Nothin', but thanks for askin'. Have a good day."

Every interaction is laced with ambiguity, laden with suspense: Do they know I am really a girl? If they don't, when will they figure it out, and what will their reaction be? I have passed through airport security with an ID that clearly states my girl name and female gender, and been waved on with a "have a nice trip, sir." The guy at the McDonald's will call me "sir" and then go through an embarrassing, apologetic spiel when he figures out my real gender. Even when I enter a women's bathroom downtown, I am looked at with skepticism and fear.

But there are a couple of things I can count on, and one is that the crack dealers in the neighborhood know I'm a girl. Perhaps they're used to more toughie-lookin' girls, and their street survival depends on keen observation. Also, a john can spot a girl-booty from a mile away.

The subway is nearly empty, the day's heavy commute yet to begin. The few of us riding are on our way to manual-labor jobs—lunch pails and hard hats, nannies and sweatshop workers. Many of us are lulled into a snooze by the rhythms of the train. We open sleepy eyes at each stop. We are the working class, the sleeping class. I put my headphones on. Mobb Deep's album *The Infamous*, all jazzy New York beats and angry, disenfranchised rhymes. In the sleepy loneliness of the morning, it makes sense.

Off the train and on the bus. Gerome is already sprawled out on one of the back seats; he gives me one of those smiles, like, we're such suckers for bein' on the bus so goddamn early. I sit across from him. "How much did ya pay?" he asks.

"What?"

"For your fare?"

"Oh, thirty-five cents—kid's fare."

"Ten cents," he says.

"How'd ya do that?"

He shrugs real nonchalant. "I think she likes me," he says, nodding toward our bus driver. She's an older black lady who seems mostly concerned with getting to the next stop, by the Quickmart, so she can get her coffee.

"I think you're high," I tell Gerome. The bus stops and our lady gets off. Gerome scoots closer to me. "Can you tell?" he asks.

"What?"

"I've been up all night." He has been working for the company for a year longer than me and half as long as he's been in the States, having come from central Mexico. He picked up driving the backhoe like a pro. It's a skill that could make him money someday, though because we are all officially "unskilled," the company pays us very little for our labor. It's the beginning of the San Francisco dot-com boom, and slowly all my friends are getting evicted. It happened to Gerome, too, and now he stays with his uncle, a coke dealer. "There were girls there, I couldn't get to sleep," he says. In a year Gerome will get busted for car theft and be sent back to the old country.

*   *   *

We arrive at the strip mall, where there are various laborers standing around, coffee in hand. Our supervisor pulls up furiously in his truck, a.k.a. the weed truck. When we are working with a big crew there are often a few choices for getting back home and every ride is different. Boss is a stoner, hence the name. My preferred ride home is the tequila truck.

John is there. He smells like vodka, which both comforts and repulses me. John is in his late forties, though we can't know for sure because he lies all the time. I like him because he has loads of incredible stories about his life—they're interesting, even if they're not true. We pile into the boss's truck and I sit in the back, between John and Gerome, so that they don't ruin their masculinity by sitting beside each other. Jeffrey is like a nineteen-year-old overgrown puppy; he fixes things well and falls a lot. He sits in the front, lookin' out for cops 'cause boss speeds like a mother. Jeffrey adjusts the piece of wood that holds the stick shift in fifth gear. They talk about *Monday Night Football* plays. A new guy gets crammed in the back of our truck, next to Gerome. He is white, kinda thuggy, probably thinks I'm a guy, probably thinks Gerome is white, 'cause he is so light-skinned, and by the end of the day he might even believe that John scored with a couple of Japanese twins when he lived in Hawaii. Gerome lays his head on my shoulder and I put my head on his head, coffee in hand. I can sleep holding on to stuff and not spill it—a coffee, a beer; it is one of the traits God blessed me with.

By 7:30 I am standing in a gravel parking lot with a sixty-pound jackhammer in my hand. Gerome drives off on the tractor with John, breeze in his hair. "See ya later, *compadres!*" he yells, and I flip him off, a very feeble comeback. I do feel sorry for him, 'cause he didn't sleep and I did, and I can still feel the sunburn from our ride home in the tequila truck yesterday.

This crazy rich lady wants a few eighty-foot palm trees in her parking lot, where nothing would ever wish to grow. It's a delicate area. Because it's by the winery, there's lots of underground piping, so we have to do a lot of it by hand. Oscar is like an ox—he works and drinks harder than anybody. He doesn't speak much English and I don't know so much Spanish, but we have a relationship based on our rides home in the tequila truck and our mutual respect for each other's hard work. He seems impressed that a girl can use a shovel. Today we are digging a gravel parking lot, with base rock, hard clay, maybe even cement if we're lucky. It's all about the compression hammer. Shovel and pickaxes for now, and we take turns with jackhammer duty. Fluorescent orange lines mark the trenches, sweeping around one of the ranch buildings. I wonder if the owner wants these trees in her parking lot so she has a shady place to park her Mercedes.

I survey the surrounding landscape. The hot sun is already starting to burn off the morning fog, revealing clear, bright blue skies and pristine, green rolling hills. I would probably think it was pretty if I wasn't hung over, or if it wasn't my job.

Boss rolls up in the truck, wearing his mirrored, I-was-a-cool-guy-in-the-eighties Oakley surfer shades. He sticks his head out the window and speaks English with a thick Spanish accent. He doesn't know Spanish, but he thinks if he speaks in broken English it will help Oscar understand him better.

"O.K. we are starting off with drainage here. The trenches are two and a half feet wide and four feet deep, everything is clearly marked, but look out for the pipes, hear me Rick? Don't break any pipes. I'll be in the shed if you have questions. *Comprende?*"

"Got a lot of paperwork today, boss?" "Paperwork" is my joke for reading the newspaper.

Boss looks unamused. "I want to see less talk and more digging," he says, kicking up gravel as he peels out of the lot.

"*Sí,* Señor Pendejo," I say.

I adjust my safety goggles. Oscar is grinning at me as if he's watching a situational comedy.

"Um, 'scuse me," I say to the new guy, "do you not remember how to warm up the compressor?" He's realized that I am a chick and is standing, shovel in hand, jaw flapped open. "Uh, I guess you should take that shovel and start clearing out some of that gravel," I say.

He is still gawking at me, like he's deciding if he should do what the woman says, or just make a run for it, into the rolling Northern California hillside, perhaps to become a mountain man of sorts, never to be heard from again.

"C'mon man, just move the gravel," I say.

He looks toward Oscar for sympathy, but Oscar—who no doubt knows what's going on—has distracted himself with the knobs and dials of the compressor. The new guy reluctantly starts shoveling the gravel into tiny piles. What's the problem? You guys have never seen a hung-over lesbian with a jackhammer before?

As the only female laborer in the company, I'd like to represent—you know, to prove something, like "girls rule!"—but my slacker mentality and general laziness keep me from being any kind of star employee. I'm just a regular working-class schmuck. I pull my weight, but sneak off to smoke weed in the port-o-potty when I get the chance. "I have to do my girl's business," I say, and then hang out in the stench, pulling off my stem and staring at the brown plastic walls with dirty Spanish words scratched into them: *"Chulo," "puto,"* alongside crude pictures of pussy and cock.

I think about screwing a lot when I'm digging. There is something about the physicality of the work—the flexing, sweat, and hard bodies, and my own shirt, which I'm not allowed to take off 'cause it'll be too distracting. Lined up on the hillside, trenching old-school chain-gang style, pickaxes flying, swinging in the rain, and the rhythm of the breath and grunts, the thud of mud moving, splashing around us, dig the holes, fill the holes, dirt, dirty jokes, base rock, gravel, sand, mud, cement.

There are times when I wish I could fit into the butch-femme paradigm; then my sexuality would make more sense to the guys. I'd have a pretty girl on my arm to kiss me and say, She's my man. But no, I'm just out here shoveling sand, dating girls that look like guys, which would make me kind of a fag. Which isn't so accepted in my line of work. Identifying as an anticapitalist art nerd doesn't really help build my machismo, either. I don't talk so much. Trying to relate stories of gender dysphoria becomes confusing, like—usually I pass as a man, except in the morning, when guys think I'm a hooker. Relating work stories to my artistic lesbian friends is usually not very effective, either—who wants to hear about the hundred yards of piping you just laid, or the keen efficiency with which you can pick up piles of sand with the backhoe? The what? What's a backhoe? Eyes glazed over, never mind. But when you are used to being the freak it almost doesn't seem so unnatural that no one gets you.

During high school I was a dishwasher at an Italian restaurant. It was all grease and steam and rancid tomato sauce. The smell coated my clothes and my very weird eighties skater haircut that was long on one side and shaved on the other. The chefs were guys and the waitresses were girls, except for one extremely charismatic gentleman waiter. The dishwashers were Mexican immigrants, and me. I watched the ladies coming through the double swinging doors with their trays, skirts swirling around, and it was like they were in some show, an opera. They came backstage to the kitchen to let us in on some dumb customer requests, then swooshed back out to the stage. There was something about them. They did the girl thing really well, and I was thinking about the tips they made. Was I always gonna be makin' $4.75? Was I gonna have to learn to wear pumps? It seemed that if I did, it would be the part of the opera where the man comes out in drag—fuckin' hilarious.

My mother was a working-class intellectual. That's what I called it. She read a lot, and worked low-paying jobs until she decided to go to library school. Now she is a library clerk. She still rents the poorly heated, ramshackle house I grew up in. I always wore combat boots, which back then was a big deal for girls in the Midwest. In the winter, after work, I would stick my half-frozen, soaking-wet, booted feet in the tiny gas oven, puff on Ma's smokes, have a shot of whiskey, wait 'till I smelled burning rubber, and take the boots out. Our house would have been condemned if the city cared, but compared to the very small Section Eight apartments next door, it seemed luxurious. The neighborhood consisted of folks raising rabbits and chickens, dope dealers who got busted monthly, and little kids sittin' on the stoop, waitin' for their folks to quit arguing. Or just waitin'. A new set of tenants would move in, a new set of guys would step to me as I walked home from school. Instinctively I puffed myself up. If you can pass as a guy you can walk independently through the world, especially at night. This I knew before I knew anything about being butch.

The liberal arts training that I received landed me into a great deal of debt instead of a secure place in the job market. In the city of San Francisco I wore button-down shirts a few times and rode the elevators of office buildings, trying to score one of those high-paying temp jobs. The woman would look at me: nervous, with a fresh buzz cut and no office experience. "I can get you a job passing out flyers," one woman said. Another woman just laughed at me. "I can probably get you a job as a day laborer," she said, looking over my résumé. I changed out of the button-down shirt on the elevator down from her office. I put on a T-shirt, feeling like a reverse Superman changing real fast into my original identity before I hit the ground floor. I imagined that I was a simple bulldagger in street clothes, but in the button-down shirt, I was "Officeman," with keen schmoozing abilities and the superhuman power to make money reproduce on its own. No one knew my real identity; I invested wisely, and I saved lots of people. I bought Ma a house. And then, *ding*, the elevator doors opened, I was back in the lobby, back on the street. I lost a day's pay for that one, having called in sick to go to the interview and listen to this chick tell me I could be a day laborer, doin' the job I already had, but for less pay.

I check out the new guy. He is shoveling gravel furiously, trying to prove himself by workin' extra hard. He might stick around, though, and if he does he might get friendly and start telling me his story, and I won't tell him my story, and he won't ask why.

Oscar works for us, week in and week out, as a day laborer. It's because he is illegal. We sneak him in. We take turns signing his week-laborer time slips under different names, and he gets paid cash. He came to this country seeking economic refuge but he cannot work under his own name. There are so many ambiguities, and yet they are always the same— like the newest guy will always buy John a beer the first Friday we get paid, because John always tells every new guy that it's his birthday. It seems like every morning my girl stumbles in thinkin' she's gonna get laid, I wake up thinkin' it's rainin', and the damn Toyota is doin' laps. A hooker looks hopefully in my direction, hopin' I'm a john.

Oscar—who thinks it's hilarious I got the new guy to work—gives me a wink and then a thumbs-up before powering up the compressor. I squeeze the handle and a surge of power releases into the hammer; I grind my teeth and think, Damn, that feels good, and sparks and tiny cement chips fly around me. I watch the flesh on my forearms jiggling, then I get the fear for a second—am I really gonna be able to do the work, to make it through the day? I think about digging, and not breaking pipes, and then I think about fucking, and the girl I left sleeping in my bed, and it's all going to be O.K.

FIGHTING

Bee Lavender

The first fight I remember, I was five years old. My uncle Anton had just married a dimpled, dark-haired girl; the church was filled with golden light streaming into my eyes, and I blinked jealously from the front row. The girl had not asked me to be in the wedding.

After the ceremony there was a cake reception in the basement of the church and my family stayed on one side of the big drafty room, sitting on folding chairs behind round folding tables. The bride's family stayed on the other side—except for the maid of honor, the bride's little sister, Susie, who had been sneaking drinks from some old man. She went from table to table in her cotton eyelet dress with yellow bows, giggling and talking to people. Susie had dark hair cut short like Dorothy Hamill's, a bowl shape on top of her head. I watched her moving around the room and wished I could have that hair, but my straggly reddish blonde hair was past my shoulders and my mother set it each night on squishy pink curlers. In the morning she combed out the curls and sprayed on hairspray. My hair fuzzed in soft curls for a few hours and then fell straight again before the middle of the day.

The flower girls were all from the bride's family, little girls in eyelet and ribbons, and I didn't want to talk to them. My Aunt Louisa held my hand and walked me over to the strange girls and introduced us. "These are

your new cousins," she said. I didn't get it; why did I need new cousins? I
had so many already, we were related to most of the town. The little girls
stared back at me. They were wearing cute white bonnets with yellow
ribbons under the chin; real brown curls trickled from under the bonnets
and all the way to their waists. They didn't say hello; they just stared.
Apparently they didn't need a new cousin either. Aunt Louisa let go of my
hand, patted me on the back, and walked away to talk to Susie. I turned
and walked away from the girls. They looked mean.

The church party broke up quickly, all the presents were loaded into a
truck, and the bride and groom made out in front of the car my dad and
some of the other grown-ups had decorated with shaving cream and tin
cans tied on with string.

Back at my grandparents' farm, the real party started, with just our
family and the neighbors and a few of the teenage friends of the teenage
married couple. The uncles had stacked cases of Budweiser on the back
porch, and Grandma Vi had cooked a big dinner of macaroni noodles and
tomato sauce with crumbled hamburger, store-bought greasy whole
chickens, and packages of flaky pull-apart rolls.

My mother brought in plates of deviled eggs, which had been stored
in our trunk during the wedding, and she stood in the kitchen laughing
and talking to her sisters as she mixed up tuna to spread on tiny pieces
of sliced rye bread. My mother was beautiful, young; she would have
been twenty-three when that party happened. She was wearing a green
velvet dress with puffy sleeves. All seven kids in her family started blonde
and ended up dark, like the relatives from Finland—dark-haired blue-
eyed people with high cheekbones, everyone with broad shoulders, the
women with soft breasts and curving hips, a good place to sit if you were
small enough to demand the privilege. I wasn't that small anymore, but
I was small enough, and my mother loved me and held me tight. I could
still sit in Grandma Vi's lap, and I could still ask my mother to carry me
when I was tired.

I played with my cousins in the sewing room, a white room with a huge
closet we used as a fort, a magical portal, and a hiding place, standing
between or behind the rows of Grandma Vi's silky polyester dresses, which

smelled of acidic perfume, Lysol, dog. The whole house smelled of dog; there was Tuta, which they said meant "girl" in Finnish, a mixed German shepherd with a happy face and waggly body. There was Boyka, which I suppose meant "boy," or was a bad translation or joke or something; he was a big red Irish setter, tall and strong enough that I could ride him like a horse. He was Anton's dog and would go to the new house with the new couple. There was Conrad, a white wolfish dog, rescued by my Uncle Frederick from an abusive home. He was friendly and sweet and known to attack anyone wearing a uniform. There was a tiny, ancient black mop of a dog named Midgie who had always been around and probably dated back to my mother's childhood. Midgie was territorial about Grandma Vi's recliner, wouldn't let us sit in it. She went everywhere we went, and Grandma would buy her ice-cream cones and hamburgers.

We played in the back room and the grown-ups sat around the house, smoking and drinking and cracking jokes at the new couple's expense. We ate off paper plates, the plain red tomato sauce seeping through, bits of food dropping off to be eaten by the dogs. People started going home, the great-aunts first, with their assorted kids and grandkids, then the teenage friends; they had other parties to go to that night. Soon it was mainly family in the house and it was late, and my mother told me to lie down on the couch, then tucked a crocheted brown and red afghan around me. My own little dog snuggled with me on the flat, dirty silk pillow stitched to commemorate a stranger's trip to a foreign port, Manila or Okinawa, the memory fades. I fell asleep listening to my mother and her brothers and sisters, all together, all laughing, Grandma Vi and Grandpa Tom and assorted husbands and wives in the dining room and kitchen.

I woke up to the sound of glass breaking, voices raised in anger. I sat up and hugged my little white dog to me, confused. My mother ran past, coming from the bathroom with towels, and said sharply, "Put on your shoes." Had I done something wrong? What was happening? I reached down for my shiny, black buckle shoes. I slipped one small foot into a shoe and was pushing the strap through the buckle when a roar and a chorus of screams made me look up, just as my uncle, the groom, came running straight at me, face red and mouth cracked open in a hideous scream, his eyes the eyes of a horror-movie maniac. His brother, the one who rescued dogs, was behind him, tattooed arm reaching forward to grab his shirt, ponytail disheveled; Grandpa Tom was there too, his hand on Anton's belt. Anton screamed a conquered-warrior scream, a victim scream, the sound of a sick and dying animal cornered and fighting back. My uncle and grandfather leapt forward at the same time, tackling Anton, and the three bodies hurtled through the air, sliding across the coffee table in front of me, pieces of their errant bodies connecting with my knees, arm, head. They slid across the coffee table and landed in a heap next to the front door, knocking over lamps, and my little dog jumped into the fray, biting at any piece of flesh he could reach.

Someone grabbed me and yanked me off the couch, and it seemed like I was flying through the rooms, carried aloft like lumber, one shoe dangling, the other lost in the fray of fighting men, grunting and pummeling each other. I screamed, "No, no, my puppy!" But whoever was carrying me ignored my screams and ran away from the fight, past the remains of supper on the big oak table, through a kitchen spattered with blood and sparkly broken glass, through the dark porch and outside. I could smell whiskey and beer and then I was standing with no coat in the yard, next to the picnic table and the sandbox, the silver dollar plants and willow tree, the bride.

She was crying, and in the dim light from the nearby chicken coop, I could see mascara streaming down her face and neck, making smudges on her white shirt. We were alone. The rest of the family was inside, and we could hear them yelling, dogs barking; but we had been set aside, sent away into the exile of the yard. My foot with no shoe on was wet from the dew on the grass, the night was cold, and I could see stars and a sliver of moon above the orchard. The bride cried and cried and I patted her arm. "It's O.K.," I said. "This doesn't happen very often."

The next fight I remember was my own. I was six years old, and I was playing in the woods across from my house, a tangled mass of blackberry bushes and salal and wild rhododendrons, evergreens shading our special places. The children of the neighborhood—not so much a neighborhood, really, just four short streets of low-income housing set down next to an abandoned city dump, on the far southern outskirts of the county—had made paths in and out of the remnants of the forest closest to our homes. We had clearings and we had hollowed logs; there were tiny winding trails and some bigger trails our dads made for dirt bikes. I was in the woods, in a clearing, on a sunny weekend day in the fall, after kindergarten started, before the rainy season.

The two red-headed girls from the yellow house, the only one with an eight-foot fence around the whole yard, were with me, along with my best friend Shanna's younger brother, Todd. Shanna was locked in her house doing chores; she was three years older than me and faced a vastly more complicated system of rules—commensurate with her status as an older kid, a fourth-grader. Todd was two years younger than me, not in school yet, a baby; but a mean-tempered baby with the whitest of white hair, dark suntanned skin, ripped denim jeans, and the top to a set of Underoos worn as a shirt.

We were playing a game where the girls were the pioneers, in wagons, trudging across the deserts and barren plains we had seen on television Westerns. It didn't occur to me then to wonder how the pioneers who went all the way west, to the Northwest, the Olympic Peninsula, the very farthest tip of the United States before it drops into the ocean, covered in a dense, mottled, cold, impenetrable rain forest, had managed their journey. Now it seems to me that the barren plains, though barren, would at least have been easier to walk across. No hacking away at scrub.

Todd was the ox, tied up with a jump rope, pulling our weary pioneer wagon as we sang songs and worried about ambush. "Faster, oxen," I called to him, tapping his bottom with the wooden handle of the jump rope. Laura and Jeanne giggled and Todd said it would take more than that to make him go faster. I tapped his bottom harder, and he stared at me with his cold baby eyes. "Is that all you can do?" he challenged me. I tapped again, harder. He laughed at me and the girls giggled. "How about this?" I asked, and hit harder. He kept laughing. I raised my arm above the soft bottom he was wiggling at me, daring me, and brought the wooden handle down with a *thwack!*

Suddenly the "ox" reared up, ropes swinging in an arc, and he wasn't a pretend animal anymore but a real one. He shoved me to the ground and pinned me, hitting and scratching as I pushed and writhed and tried to get away. The red-headed girls had stopped giggling and were standing there with their mouths open, and then they ran away, not to get help, but to hide behind their high fence. I shoved at Todd but I was shocked and scared, and he was a solid boy.

We rolled in the dirt and then he had his hands on my ears, on my pretty new earrings, and he clutched and yanked as hard as he could, and then his face was close to mine and I could feel my ear lobe tear and I started to cry and then his mouth was on my cheek, his teeth digging in, ripping the skin, the skin of my face and my ear, and I screamed and pushed and knocked him away, running for home without looking back.

I had blood on my face, blood on my neck; the earring had been ripped forward all the way through the lobe, leaving me not with a tiny piercing but with a large jagged hole. My mother tried to ask me what happened, tried to wipe off the blood, but I was sobbing and my nose and mouth filled with mucous and I started to hiccup and I couldn't say much except "Todd hurt me."

There was a knock at the door. My mother went to answer it, and I could hear the voice of Todd's mother; she was yelling, and she had Todd with her. I ran to the pantry and hid in the very lowest cupboard and pulled the sliding hollow door shut behind me, cowering in the dark. I could hear Cindy telling my mother the story of what happened; she made Todd pull down his pants to show a red mark from the jump rope. My mother listened and then said, "Well, my kid has her ear ripped half off, and bite marks on her face." My mother didn't sound angry, just stiff and formal, as if this comment was the end of the discussion, the bill is in the mail, good-bye. She was good friends with this woman, whose daughter was my best friend. We went places together, to the zoo, inner tubing, camping on the coast.

After Cindy left, my mother slid the pantry door open. "Come out," she said, and she didn't sound happy.

"Next time," she said, "you have to hit back."

*   *   *

The women in my family hit back. Sometimes they hit first. Not usually in
a provocative way, not to start a fight—but in the middle of a fight, when
the rage over some enormous transgression boiled over. It's easy enough to
break the rules when you live not only in poverty, but in the lowest dregs
of working poverty, too poor to feed your family but not poor enough to
receive government benefits, when you're a family living on a boy-man's
salary for delivering newspapers or pumping gas or part-time work in the
forest. Often, there would be an argument over something the boy-man
bought. A model car, a magazine, tickets to a movie, a special treat—and
that money should have gone toward a loaf of bread. They would argue,
then scream, and the boy-man would have a shaking tantrum. These men,
even the violent ones, were just boys who broke the rules. If a fight started
in the car, it usually ended with the man dropped off on the side of the
road, kicked out to walk home or bum a ride off a stranger.

But sometimes, someone would raise a hand and hit. Then they would
fall on each other, stand back up, fall back down, go waltzing around the
room in a macabre dance of violence (but they did not know how to waltz,
so perhaps it was a square dance, a do-si-do), while I sat in the crackly
green reclining chair and watched Westerns on television.

Nobody hit *me*, not even as a measure of discipline. My cousins were
cuffed routinely; someone was always threatening to cut a switch; smacks
fell down like rain. But I was absolutely protected within this family,
because my mother would not let anyone touch me, and because I was a
bleeder. My nosebleeds were frequent and copious—I could soak a towel
or fill the sink basin just from riding in a car or reading too long or falling
asleep in an awkward position. If I felt sad, I coughed up blood. Growing
up, I was usually sick, curled up with a blanket and an infected organ, ear,
throat—recuperating perpetually, watching television and reading books.
People had fights, they hit each other, and I was never touched.

I saw fights between my Aunt Louisa, the baby of the family, a teenager
still with short hair and David Bowie T-shirts, and her husband, my
favorite, who drove a VW van and wore purple high-top sneakers with
plaid bell-bottoms. His parents had a lake cabin, an impossible luxury, and
we used to float around the lake on inner tubes, lazily stroking the murky

water, and then climb up the steep stairs to the A-frame cabin where three boys spent summers in a perfect—sitcom-perfect, like *Hazel* or *Father Knows Best*—childhood. Aunt Louisa used the baby's diaper bag to hide their stash of drugs, and I know that when they broke up, someone hit someone else, and my aunt's eardrum was punctured, but it was never clear to me why my now ex-uncle was the bad guy. He always seemed so nice, and my aunt, well, there was the story about the time she wouldn't stop kicking one of her sisters in the car and the car went in a ditch and they ended up pummeling each other in the middle of a busy road.

It was understood, though never discussed, that the habitual, reflexive violence in our family was an expression of strength, that we were not abused but merely querulous. We were the strong ones, the victorious, and the women in the family were to be honored for their ability to fight. The women whispered about the new bride's younger sister, Susie, who had married a man with a moustache and mean eyes. He hit Susie and she just put her hands across her eyes, crying. Susie showed up with bruises on her arms, black eyes, and a big pregnant belly. My mother and her sisters said that if she couldn't protect herself she should leave, or, failing that, kill him; they nodded and agreed that they would never let a man get away with that shit.

When her baby was still in diapers she was pregnant again and she tried to leave, but the man broke down the door and beat Susie up, left her bleeding on the floor, took his son, and disappeared forever.

Some fights were so legendary, discussed so often, it was easy to imagine you had been a witness even if you weren't born yet when the event occurred. My Aunt Signe, my mother's oldest sister, had a wretched husband, the worst kind of bad imaginable. She had a good job as a secretary in the shipyard, and one day in the middle of an argument he swept up all of her work clothes and took them outside. He threw the clothes in their muddy driveway and then drove back and forth over them with his car. When he came back inside he was laughing and he picked up a bottle of wine and raised it to his lips for a drink. She smacked that bottle into his mouth, shattering teeth and glass—bone and blood and glass and wine spilling forward across the kitchen table as he screamed.

One day they had a fight about dog food and he hit her and she grabbed a knife and chased him out of the house. He ran down the driveway and she got in her station wagon and knocked him down and drove over him, grinding him into the mud and gravel, just like he had driven over her beige pantsuits, permanent-press skirts, blouses with ruffled collars.

It didn't kill him; we believed he was too wicked to die. We whispered, "Too bad she didn't use the truck" as he passed through the dining room on his way to torment someone in the living room, hobbling on crutches, stinking of motor oil and whiskey. Of course, my aunt would have gone to prison, which would have been bad, because she was the respectable one, with a nice hairdo and a job in the shipyard, and she was smart and funny.

One bright, sunny day I was driving across the Tacoma Narrows Bridge, Mt. Rainier on the horizon and sailboats far below. I was wearing an electric-blue mini-dress. My hair was long and blond, held back with a chiffon scarf, and my legs were covered with laddered tights, black boots to my knees. I had a boyfriend of rare beauty sitting next to me, and we were driving to Seattle to see a band called Pure Joy.

I reached out to change the radio station and he smacked my hand away. Without pause for thought, my hand curled into a fist and my arm jerked back, up, and with vicious force connected with the face of this pretty boy. Without forethought or planning, without losing control of the car hurtling at fifty miles per hour over a high bridge, I hit him as hard as I could. He held both hands to his face. His voice was muffled and he started to cry. "You broke my nose," he said.

This was neither the first nor the worst of our many fights. After the episode on the bridge, I would like to say, that was the end, the moment, the signifier. But my courage, the purest and most valiant part of me, did not match my wisdom. I tried to break up with him after awhile, and I told him we had broken up, but he didn't believe me. More important, I had broken one of the most important rules of those who practice domestic violence: I hit above the neck. The arm that struck the blow would have to pay. After that day on the bridge, every time we fought, he grabbed my wrist, twisted, shoved—shoved my elbow into a wall with a dull thud, or punched the lee of the joint with a sharp pop. On cold mornings or when the season changes, my arm gets numb, and sometimes there is a flash along the nerve that runs between the smallest finger and the elbow, reminding me of those teenage games.

We were in love, and it was a passionate and enormous love, and the dialectic of our family lives (for his mirrored my own) never taught us how to act any differently, to restrain ourselves, to enjoy the quiet things in life. He touched my scars and said that I was beautiful. We were young and reckless and the sex was good and the laughs were fine and it was delightful, addictive, to be alive.

We broke up eventually out of boredom, because we wanted to kiss other people. My teenage love saga ended with a different boy, years later, an honorable boy inevitably corrupted by the reality of life in a hard poor town and the dangers that befall children when their mothers are not vigilant in protecting them, body and soul. This story ends with a 9-mm handgun held at my right temple, as I looked into the eyes of a boy who would never have hit me. This was our contract, we had figured out that much: He would never hit me, nor would I touch him in anger.

But we were both damaged by our short, fast lives and the inescapable events that brought us to this particular clean moment, standing in a shabby white kitchen of a dank basement apartment, dirty dishes on the counter, school papers scattered everywhere.

In a different kind of story he would be portrayed as shaking with rage, flushed with power, blustering and roiling with emotion. But in real life he was steady and determined, the barrel of the gun pressing against my skin an admonition, a benediction; and I neither doubted his intent nor his ability and willingness to act.

He would argue, "But you had a knife," and this is true. I had a good knife, a sharp and lethal knife, pressed to his belly, and knew how to use it. Even if I couldn't survive this fight, I could inflict damage.

I looked at his round young face, pale and freckled, at his brown eyes as he decided exactly when to pull the trigger, and remembered all the other moments of rage, the other fights I had won or lost, and felt a despair deep as any mountain lake. I thought, "This can be the end of all the fighting, it would be so easy." Simply being alive had been such a terrible war of attrition, I had survived by a narrow margin, and I could have chosen to do so many other things with my hard-won victory. I could have traveled, or learned to sing, could have done anything in the world, and I had chosen this boy and this moment. I had used up all of myself and ended up no more than a mile from my childhood home. I was just on the far side of the same forest. The rage emptied out of me and I was calm. "Put it down," I said quietly, and I continued looking into the madness of his eyes until his eyelids fluttered and closed, and he stepped away.

All of the people in these stories managed to grow up and settle down and stay together, and eventually, to stop fighting, and still love each other. Or they chose death. But even with the example of many long marriages, fractious but no longer violent, or the wretched uncle eventually tamed and consigned to a wheelchair, or the honest and simple suicides and murders, I could not or would not move beyond the moment with the gun at my temple. That was the end of a specific relationship, but also the end of my rage. It was the last fight.

I walked away from my lover, my family. I stepped out of the diorama, tore up the placard, walked away from the box that contained the scenes of battle. I moved away and started over with a new identity; with a new family; with scores of friends, chosen carefully.

One of my young friends was confiding in me recently about her problems with her lover, and wanted advice, or at least a little perspective. I shrugged and said, "Maybe you should date someone who had a happy childhood." This is advice I inflicted on myself after the fighting stopped, and ten years of decency has proved worth the effort (and just as exciting). It is not easy, it is in fact harder, to be vulnerable, to be kind.

I'm still attracted to damaged people, the grown-up children of violence, the people who keep secrets and show off lies. But I keep them at a certain safe distance, and politely decline to play. I have a strict and repressive code of conduct for myself, and I will not fight, nor debate, nor will I

even speak to people who might cause me to fall again, to take that reckless, thoughtless slide down into rage.

Those of us who grew up fighting know each other without telling
these stories; we can smell it, maybe, or perhaps see it in the way a hand
rests on a table. Maybe we hold our bodies differently; maybe the secret
crosses our faces before we even know that we have given it away. I do not
consciously try to convey information with my body, but I've never been
panhandled or harassed on the street. Nobody has ever asked me out on a
date or flirted with me in a social setting. I can walk through a large crowd
and people move swiftly out of my way.

In this adult life I have had only two opportunities to fight. The first
happened several years ago, on a dark night with no moon or stars, a
cold night. I had put my baby into the back of the car, buckled the car
seat, and was about to get in when I sensed danger. I turned around and
a man had materialized, not near the car, but actually standing within
the curve of the door. He reached out with both arms and I pulled back
my fist and he saw, through the scrim of light from the car, the expression on my face. He pulled his hands back, held them in front of his face,
jumped back a foot, stumbled, and apologized before running away into
the darkness.

Another day, a dry autumn day, I arrived home with my children and
unlocked the door. The living room looked strange; something was
missing, and I could see through a doorway that my study had been
searched; clothes I had left stacked on the desk were strewn across the
floor, wires pulled out of the wall. Standing in the living room I could see
that the back door was still locked. I sent the children back outside. I
grabbed the nearest possible weapon, a large metal flashlight, and ran up
the stairs. My only thought was to find and hurt the person who had
invaded my home, who might have hurt us. It wasn't until I had checked
all the closets and stood next to the broken window, the route of entry and
escape, that I realized what a foolish choice I had made. My instinct was
not to get help, but rather to attack.

This is my meditative discipline: a constant wakeful awareness of
danger. My blood contains the secrets, the knowledge of hospital corridors

and the threat of injury. I can only offer the most obvious lesson I have learned: that anger feeds rage and rage breeds violence and that people who allow anger to dwell in their bodies and minds perpetuate the cycle. But I'm not didactic about it; I'm not testifying. I don't really care enough to convince anyone to change. Life is complicated, and if I hadn't known how to defend myself, I would not have survived. I just want to keep my small family safe and to stay here, laughing, until it is time to go.

SCHOLARSHIP BABY

Leah Lakshmi Piepzna-Samarasinha

"You got one ticket to ride, kid. Don't blow it."

—my mother

I blew it.

Scholarship baby, ticket-to-ride holder, geto supastar, grassroots intellectual: So much of who I am is about being my mother's exceptional daughter. Is about getting my first scholarship at age eight.

Proposition 21/2 cut taxes and destroyed Massachusetts's public school system, all the teachers under age fifty got fired, and my mama had me in the admissions office of the local one-horse K–12 private school before I could blink. Her voice changed in there, just the way it did when the phone company was on the line. I was so bright and exceptional, so different. She wore her best Filene's Basement and smiled just right. I got in and stayed till I was eighteen, and it worked; I'd rocked my way to three APs and a $25,000 scholarship to NYU. I was the smart kid in big brown plastic glasses and factory-outlet shoes. I was not gonna be a hairdresser on black beauties like my cousins. Maybe we were back in Wormtown 'cause it was the only place my mother could afford a house, but she was gonna keep snapping at me whenever I said "Wuh-stah," and keep buying the best secondhand cars she could afford.

But what happens when you don't grow up to bust outta your hometown into the stars? When you're the one who gets away, but you don't? 'Cause if you fuck up your one chance, that's it. Right?

I'm in Toronto, I'm twenty-three. There's a national border between me and my family for a reason. And I am not the lawyer or doctor my parents dreamed was going to cement the deal. I'm still on a visitor's visa and can't access the free health care we'd dream about back home. We knew folks who'd drive up to Montreal and scam free prescriptions for Seldane meds from the clinics, but that was before welfare reform, tip lines, and photos on the health cards. I'm sick. I'm in a fucked-up house that has a back yard but is under the power lines and by the tracks. I can't afford rent or food. I'm working under the table. Make no long-distance calls so the phone won't be cut off. Use my eyes and smile and voice to make Immigration like me. I'm passing as a slumming, middle-class college kid who's breezy about the rent to my landlady. I listen to the train chugging by. Walk everywhere. Start eating meat again—for one more dollar, shwarma goes farther than falafel. I don't use social services. Not gonna look good if I get called for that interview. I've got one shot.

"Our generation's screwed," this boy I met on the fifty-dollar Toronto–Montréal van said. "We all grew up thinking nobody was gonna ever make money."

Nobody's really rich in Wormtown. The ones who think they are own used-car lots and outlet-mall stores, but damn, they're doing better than the rest of the town. And of course there are the petty nobility: the folks who go to the Worcester Club, who showed up on some tag-along to the fuckin' *Mayflower*.

The whitest people in the world live in New England. In the New Haven bus station bathroom, on our way to a gig at Yale to do a performance about class for the rich South Asian kids having a conference about it, I see them for the first time in years—the fine-boned blondes who look like Jill on *The Practice*, the ones I grew up closer to, big Irish-Polish faces, big hair, first acid-wash and now booty jeans.

Fumes from Norton, the world's largest manufacturer of ceramic tile, blew over the school. When the wind blew the right way it stank of garbage or burning tar. Every year a teacher got either breast cancer or alopecia, and we got used to watching their hair drop out bit by bit during class. Worcester is the only place I've ever heard of where working-class folks try to afford bottled water and it's 39¢ a gallon, just for the town. The second girl I kissed, who grew up in Leominster (known for the uranium that leaked into the water), found out she had cervical cancer at thirty, during the mandatory pelvic for egg donation—her first health care in ten years. All the downtown was abandoned: Funland, the toy store with the big rotting clown murals that'd gone bust; Union Station, back when working-class cities had department stores and strollable downtowns, now with trees growing up through the roof. Half-cracked parking lot and thirteen-story high-rises with all the windows busted out.

My mom had tried to flee Worcester. She made it partway. All the way to two master's degrees on scholarship, at night, at Anna Maria College and Assumption College, little shit colleges no one had heard of. All the way to getting a Fulbright to Uganda to study then, when the Idi Amin government expelled whites from the country, to London. All the way from being the one girl in her high school class to go to college. Everyone else pregnant, working in the mills, or married. Webster, Massachusetts, in 1956 was a long way from having any respect for nerdy intellectual girls. The only reason she got to go is because a teacher pulled her aside and was shocked that she wasn't college-bound, called up the registrar at Worcester State, and got her in. She worked at Nectarland Ice Cream parlor and in the office at the textile mill while she was in college, made a couple thou a year after she graduated. But she was a teacher.

My mama found herself back in Worcester because class is a hard thing to shake unless you're the strongest and the fastest and jettison everything to survive. And even if you're willing to strip off your family and your history, you might end up like she did—finally married at thirty-two to an exotic Sri Lankan bumming around Europe, who, it turned out, didn't have the university education he claimed on forms. My dad used his "more British than the British" accent and lovely manners to scam his way into a series of midlevel administration jobs, only to be fired mysteriously from each one. They moved back to the States, the economy crashed; they moved back to Worcester, where you could buy a house even if you were broke. It was the place my mom had spent all her life trying to flee.

But she never let me forget that she had almost made it. Halfway. A foot in. Not knowing upper-class people, not liking them, but studying them. Teaching them there is one accent for home and one for being out in the world. Teaching me to be bright and exceptional. I had a job. I was gonna get all that free money, get in to a good school 'cause I was brilliant, and move on up. I was not going to fall. You fall and you get stuck forever, in the pit of nowhere people that don't matter. But we hate the rich kids; they don't know anything real, anything about life. We ride shotgun. It's a mindfuck.

My light brown skin and green eyes are part of what makes me a good case. My mom works that too. I'm not classified as one of the "minority students." It's more like I'm seen by admissions as the kid who is a quarter "something"—a drop for garnish, but not enough to be an "issue."

In classes with the blond, pale WASPs only New England can produce, it's different. It's about being ugly. I was never called "dothead" or "spook," but "ugly": ugly being brown, kinky hair; dark skin; glasses; height; tits and hips and blood in fifth grade; leg and armpit hair thick and curling black. Just ugly. Ugly doesn't look good in eighties discount-barn clothing, powder blues and pinks, acid wash; ugly doesn't look good in big hair, hairspray, and bangs. Ugly is too smart, reads all the time, likes school.

We would drive down 290 to T.J. Maxx, where we would slowly, methodically, go through the whole store. A four-hour job. You look at every piece there 'cause only four will be doable, not trashy looking. The only Brooks Brothers suit on triple discount. Navy blue, black, taupe, nothing too colorful, one pair of outlet shoes. When I'd gone to public school I wore the same shirts from Zayre's or Caldor everyone esle wore.

Siobhan, my best friend from grades three to five, and I were the two scholarship kids, the first ones. An experiment. Her mom kept her last name and didn't give a shit. They were French Canadian. Siobhan was dark like me and had her own room in the basement of their tiny tract house out in Quabbin Hills, where every one of the bedrooms had two or three bunk beds for all the new kids who kept coming. Siobhan's room was Foxfire library books, fantasy board games, and the weeds we dried when we were playing out in the backyard—the yard that was acres of weeds and trees.

I remember my mother walking through Cambridge on the Saturday trips we would make every six weeks. The routine never varied. We would hit Urban Outfitters in the morning to look at outfits I could never afford to buy, then Bertolucci's or Uno's for pizza, then one of Cambridge's many bookstores to gorge. One book. We'd look, not buy, but we went every six weeks without fail. I remember walking through all the people who were intellectuals, my mother's dreamy eyes. I remember her stopping outside a fancy boutique window to say, reverently, "The Beaujolais Nouveau has come in," longing. My parents never would be able to afford Boston. Not without admitting they had the money they had and getting housing in a neighborhood—maybe a little poor, brown around the edges or at the heart—that also reflected who they really were.

I always imagined I would go to Harvard. Walk those brick sidewalks, go to all those bookstores, be with all the truly smart people. "You have to begin thinking how to sell yourself," the admissions person announced. Cathy and I slouched in our seats. Cathy was Polish. She had wispy blond fine hair permed and banged around her face, skirt a little too tight. A public school kid. After she'd tried to befriend the jock girls and was rebuffed, with a look of resignation she came to sit at our table. She had been popular at her old school, had had a lot of boyfriends. Still did, but also put Sinead pictures up and aggressively clipped Nike ads about motivating young women in sports. We both knew "things to put on applications" were crucial. You start grooming yourself in eighth grade, if not before. You have to be brilliant early or you won't get in the next brilliant level of classes, won't be recommended for things, will not get accepted into good schools.

The track starts in grade school and you can never fall off. Falling off means falling into the pit of normal people, the ones who torment you or the ones like your cousins. Annie and CiCia are cutting hair, dropping out of Framingham State, doing pills and acid and booze and, occasionally, heroin. They are in their mid-thirties and they are not leaving. Decked out

in the finest artsy wear Worcester can offer, they are still trapped—by loy-
alty, by letting their feelings keep them from getting that A. Doesn't matter if you're fucked up. Get the union card: the degree.

But how the fuck do you get the degree? I thought once I got there it
would be easy. The other freaks and me, we would all be there. But working-
class equals unenlightened, dumb, abused, stuck. Right?

It takes a middle-class life to believe you can write for a living. It takes parents who will pay your rent, bail you out, buy you nice consumer gear and
electronics, and make sure you have groceries, so you can score those connections. My mother tried to give that to me, but she didn't know quite how.
There was a lot of magical thinking going on. You go there and if you're
good, you get it! If you can't figure it out, well, "I dunno, Leah, how do you
expect me to know?" She was small and shabby, shy and fierce. I could see
her holes at the end; they hurt. She was not shining and clean and she could
not hold on to her pride. She spent too much time trying to hide what she
was. Oh, what a strange world she had let me believe in.

I want to be an activist. How murderously she looked at me when I said
that. But she wasn't quite sure I was wrong, either. My career should be something I loved, something that allowed me to always have health insurance,
something that was creative, something that was secure. Plant genetics or
nonprofit, maybe; anyway, something with letters after my name. Grad
school? Financial aid was taken away in the nineties, no more free money.

It makes me think a lot about class and activism and how they got me
here. I think about the folks who are all creamy over their fantastic
activist jobs and the weird promise of being well paid for the *revolution*.
I think about how my mother raised me totally on the myth that I would
be the one to get away, that I would scholarship my way outta town and
go to Harvard and become a plant geneticist or something, that working-
class ticket to ride of "you will never have to hustle again." And at the
same time, saying and modeling the view that the system's fucked, everything's fucked, it's not what it says it is, any of it, so find a safe niche and
hide until you can retire. Don't believe in the possibility of more 'cause
you'll just get screwed.

It's a class thing. She knew that the rich kids' social justice movements would just overwork and underpay her. And she was right. At the same time, she was so focused on passing as "money" that she couldn't talk about any of this shit up front. I didn't wanna be cynical like that. Her eyes would narrow, she'd get so mad when I'd tell her I was gonna get some great activist job. And she was right, too. Kind of.

I ran away 'cause I was an incest orphan and was broke and undocumented. But I ran to the crack of twenty-dollars-an-hour part-time social justice jobs in a country that's still a welfare state. (I had no idea such things existed. Get paid fourteen dollars an hour doing feminist anti-oppressive anti-psychiatry counseling at a women's centre with paid breaks and sick days? *Dawg.*)

And since I hustled in on a useless degree meant for girls with more privilege than me, I do better than the other assholes. I help folks make it through the maze 'cause I was in it. I give out phone numbers for free counseling and rent banks like crack, like candy. I give a shit. And I am still part of a social control system where reporting to Children's Aid is mandatory, where being too much of a "client" ain't cool, unless you want to be a "Look! I made it too!" street-kid-to-social-work-lady success story. The nonprofit activist heaven where "underprivileged" kids rise through our anti-oppression gospel, get jobs, are saved. Often, unfortunately, they cannot become just like us, and stay "clients." A different species. One the jobs depend on. How do "activists" who don't have a daddy to fund them subsidize our way through life without falling into wage-slaving, working at shit that sucks up our lives? Is it possible to create enough nonprofit jobs to employ all the "at-risk youth" in the world? And is this really as far as we want to go?

I want to tell my mom that there are other options, between beauty and assimilation, failing and being shit. That life don't give us a lot of choices, but the choices are bigger than she thought. Not 'cause this is a land of opportunity, but because this is a land of hustle, chaos, and a free market that constantly mutates what it allows. I'll get my words in print, but I won't always use the right accent to stay there.

We used to steal bricks out of construction sites when I was a kid. Go out at night and load them up. We made over that back yard to look like something nice, something in *Family Circle*. I want to tell her: That's my way. Beauty out of nothing, Ma, with a little more than you had. Twenty dollars in the drawer, friends and prayer for the hard times. We need a lot of tickets to ride, a lot of chances. I didn't make it like you thought, but I made it another way. And I'm still exceptional, along with all the others. Beauty and brilliance right here.

SOMETHING FROM NOTHING

Shawna Kenney

Nothing.

My sister swears she doesn't remember a single thing about our childhood. I remember specific details of every photo I see of us, when it was taken and exactly how I felt posing. I have one of me on my second birthday, sitting next to her with my hand on her baby carrier. I'd plopped down beside her on Grandpa's round rag rug seconds before the shot, feeling quite big-sisterly, like I knew it was forever my job to "betect" her, this little being, from everything.

There is one of us a couple of years later taking a bath, me smiling coquettishly at the camera, her looking down into the Mr. Bubble–foam, the two of us safe together in the belly of the white ceramic lion-pawed tub-beast. Minutes later Mom would lift us out individually, drying and powdering our little bodies with undivided attention. This was well before we knew the word "project" could mean anything other than something you made with paste and construction paper, or that our kingdom was a place people whispered about and where some cab drivers refused to go. It was in these unhurried moments I felt most loved.

For fun we bounced between playing "Kathy and Judy"—our favorite game of "betending" to be coffee-slurping, fake-cigarette-smoking, agitated moms with always absent good-for-nothing husbands to complain about—and playing school, fooling around with clay or playing freeze-tag with the neighborhood kids. I don't tell too many people about the game of "barbecue" I instigated, which involved everyone getting a stick, poking at a pile of old dog poop as if it were meat on a grill, and voilà—a "barbecue." The game usually ended with us chasing each other around, screaming, *"Gonna put it on youuuuuuu!"* We had no back yard and had never been to a real barbecue, but Barbecue was our game—a secret the adults could know nothing about. Thanks to my dad's sense of adventure, we also enjoyed weekend fishing, day trips to local parks, and my favorite—visits to whatever garage he was working at to play "mechanic's assistant." Both my sister and I had learned the difference between a wrench and a hammer by age four, and a flathead versus Phillips screwdriver by five. I learned to keep this quiet after one time in second grade when, playing hangman, the kids couldn't figure out my word. I'll never forget their looks of suspicion and disgust when I revealed it to be "crankshaft." I didn't know exactly what it was, but I knew how to spell it.

Later we learned that Dad made lopsided, too-loose pigtails when Mom had to be at work early. We learned daddies were strong. I remember my dad lying prostrate with arms outstretched, each of us standing stick-straight in the palm of his hand while he lifted us up into the air. We were wide-eyed and giggly at his Superman-like strength. One year for Christmas, Santa Claus brought us a child-sized wooden table with four matching chairs, from then on referred to as "the little table." Dad bought Mom a Mr. Coffee, which started an argument about them not being able to afford such a luxury. She demanded that he return it. Words got louder and louder, and my sister and I scooted into the small space under the couch like we did during thunderstorms. The argument ended with our dad throwing one of the new little chairs against the wall, sticks of wooden shrapnel flying everywhere. He brought the coffeemaker back; my parents kissed and made up; but the "little table" remained a three-seater, perfect for me, my sis, and one doll-baby, but forever a reminder of how Superman could change into the Hulk in a heartbeat.

I was in third grade when I noticed another weakness in my father—what an obstacle words were for him. Studying for a spelling test, I asked him to help, instead of my mom. I took the list and asked him to spell "elephant." He used an "f." I'll never know if he was pulling my leg, but later when I told my mom in private horror, she laughed and agreed that Dad was "an awful speller." From then on I noticed that he always did the bills, while Mom was "the letter-writer." Though only educated to the tenth grade herself, she was always writing a letter to the editor about some injustice or preparing job bids for my father.

My favorite piece in our old photo albums is a yellowed newspaper clipping of my father and his two brothers in Navy uniforms, with the caption "Kenney Boys Home for Christmas." It was an allowance made during the war thanks to my mom's letter-writing campaign to the governor of New York and the president, based on some law forbidding all male members of a family to be away at war at the same time. My father's handwriting still looks like my childhood scrawls—tiny, illegible hills and valleys of inky, incomplete letters smashed together, perhaps to hide his bad spelling.

Our white kitchen floors, which smelled of bleach, were "clean enough to eat off of," my mom always said, and sometimes we did, when we had a full house. I remember thinking that elbow macaroni with tomatoes thrown in was food fit for kings, and that Mom making Popsicles with Kool-Aid in ice-cube trays was a damn genius summer treat. I liked picking at the peeling corners of our cracked linoleum, but my mom yelled at me to stop if she saw me, saying, "That bastard landlord is supposed to fix that soon." I thought "bastard" was a term of endearment back then, since Gramps sometimes half-yelled, half-laughed, "Get down off the countertops, ya bastards!" while we raided his cupboards with our cousins. We played for hours with the neighborhood kids, all equals in the red brick jungle and patches of grass. The same brick jungle my mom grew up in. Stella, the deaf lady next door who sometimes yelled out the window at us in her low nasal voice for "being too rough," used to yell at her, too.

Shane Matzeo had no dad, but he had Monopoly-like plastic money to buy stuff with at the corner store. I wanted it, too, but my mom got mad when I asked. "That's welfare. Your parents work," she said. Shane was my age and sometimes my unofficial boyfriend. We touched the tips of our tongues together on the front step once, because he said that's how you kiss. We giggled afterward and promised not to tell. He had a little sister named Rachel, same age as mine, and we four played together a lot. Once, when playing Monster, Shane was "it" and chased my sister through his house until she put her arm through the glass front door. We all went to the hospital and she got fifteen stitches, so we weren't allowed to play with the Matzeo kids for awhile.

Jason Spanelli spent summers and holidays with his grandparents down the street, not exactly in the housing development, but close enough to play with us. He was a fat kid with a crush on my sister. The neighborhood whispered about his grandparents being "family," because they had a new car every other week and always paid for everything in cash. Their house was a hangout for his whole extended family, and they always offered you food the minute you stepped through the door. "Sausage and peppers? Some lasagna, Honey? Did you eat?" his grandma would say, coming at you with full steaming plates. Even if you told her you had, she made you have a piece of cake or a "no-thank-you" helping. Mom said she didn't care if they were mafia—"They're still good people," she said. "They brought us food and gave me rides everywhere when I was pregnant with you and your dad was overseas, and I'll never forget that." Plus, they were Catholic and went to our church, so she liked that, too. We were always allowed to play with Jason.

Mindy had more Barbies than anyone, because she had a sister who was fifteen years older who passed down all her Barbies and Barbie clothes. She also had the Dream Machine, Dream House, Corvette, an Easy-Bake Oven, It's Sew Easy, the Snoopy Sno-Cone Machine, Shrinky Dinks, and that Operation game. Her toys were powerful currency when she didn't get her way. "Welllllll, if I can't be teacher today, you can't borrow my Barbie disco outfit overnight," she'd say, and eventually someone would give in, usually my sister. Mindy's things were all she had going for her.

Gramps lived next door with Grandma, who was sent away to the funny farm for "nerves" before I was born. I don't know what made her so nervous, but it had something to do with the hysterectomy she had after having my Uncle Chuckie, who "wasn't quite right in the head," according to most people. Since then Grandma hadn't been right either, and she had been in and out of this funny farm, which seemed like a great place because when she came home for holidays she brought lots of mosaic ashtrays and other art projects she'd made. She never talked much, just sat chain-smoking calmly with her legs crossed all ladylike, but the top leg or foot was always bouncing up and down furiously. I think this was the "nerves." One time she drank almost a whole bottle of beer my dad had set down, and everyone freaked out. "Frances, you know better! It'll kill you with your medicine!" my grandpa screamed. She laughed and kept on bouncing that leg.

Our cousins lived in a real house down the street—seven kids in one family, so there was always someone to play with there: Bobby, Greggy, Shelly, Sherry, Cindy, Butchie, Mikey. In that order. My Uncle Butch died in a car accident when Cindy and I were six. I sat in the car with my dad during the funeral. It was raining hard and I wanted to go up to the grave site with my mom and cousins, but I was too young. I did get to go to the wake, where there was lots of food and crying and laughing, old ladies I didn't know kissing and hugging on me and my sister. Uncle Butch and his friend had been driving drunk, too fast. Partying, as usual. He wouldn't have wanted anyone crying, everyone said. This was the day I learned the word "decapitated."

We never did end up at that mysterious "poorhouse" Gramps was always talking about. We were spared the labels of "homeless," or worse, "stinky." Even if we were wearing our cousins' hand-me-downs, one weekend being dragged to the St. Vincent de Paul Society to serve soup or hand over our own hand-me-downs was enough to prove that there were people worse off than us, and that they didn't all live in China.

Last year I did some readings in the United Kingdom. I stayed at the British Library one whole day, giddy with the idea of *me* looking at the original manuscripts of *Rikki-Tikki-Tavi*, *Finnegans Wake*, *Jane Eyre*. My first reading was in Chatham, east of London. I took the train out to

Basildon and a sales rep took me around to four chain bookstores to sign stock. The bookstore people were really nice. South-By-Sea looks like the British version of Coney Island, a town next to a run-down amusement park on the water. I was walking around and thinking how lucky little ol' me was to be there, thinking how I'm from nowhere, never thought I'd go anywhere, how people from nowhere sometimes get stuck and sometimes break out, when I stumbled on a cobblestone and skinned my knee. I ripped my cute new black striped tights, and later, while gently pulling them out of the blood and rocks embedded in my leg, the words of my parents crept into my head—"Can't have nothin'!"—a phrase sputtered whenever anything of meaning or value was destroyed, as though we were destined to never have anything "nice."

These words were most often blurted when someone else in our neighborhood stole or ruined something of ours. Later, when we moved from the projects, the phrase was uttered less and less often. My parents must have known it would be hard to "have anything" living among others who had nothing. Dog eat dog. Poor stealing from the poor. It happened sometimes, and it did seem especially cruel and unexpected. You expected the poor to steal from the rich, the rich to tax or exploit the poor, the rich to steal from one another (or else how would they be rich?), but people with nothing taking a little something from other people with nothing? Insulting. Painful. Just wrong.

My sister might not remember "Can't have nothin'," but she remembers the feeling. She has a new condo, which she can't wait to show me, she says. She swipes a card and we walk through an Italian-marbled lobby, down soft, salmon-colored carpeting, and then are whisked up in silent, jetlike elevators. We walk through a winding maze of halls, passing no one. She unlocks the door and waves me in to a catalog-perfect, neat-as-a-pin, color-coordinated living room. There are gray marble kitchen countertops, fake flowers in a slender vase on a glass-topped table in the breakfast nook, perfectly arranged photos of perfectly smiling people on a shelf. There's an old one of me. Price stickers are still on the backs of some of the frames. The bedroom is immaculate. Headboard matches the dresser, big fluffy pillows on top of a big down comforter. Not a shoe peeks out from under the bed. Not a hint of make-up lies around the bathroom sink. Everything is as it should be.

It's like a display model, like one of the many little homes with minimal furniture and fake televisions we looked at when our parents went house-shopping in our teens. It looks like no one lives there until she pulls out four pairs of black pants she just bought. She pulls them from a closet full of similar black pants. But these are designer, she tells me. They still have the tags on them. They were expensive but she got them for a good deal, she says. She just paid $500 to have her hair straightened. She tells you the cost of everything because she wants you to know she can have it. In her mind, she has everything. I used to hate her for wanting it.

The only questions she and my parents ask me these days seem to be about things I've bought or can't afford to buy. Are you ever going to be able to buy a house? Don't you need a new car? Do you have health insurance yet? I think they think I have nothing.

I still can't believe my sister doesn't remember anything about the old days. She is in all of my mental snapshots, and when I dig them up, I feel the unintentional camaraderie of poverty, the little pieces of kindness in humanity when conditions weren't ideal. It's my definition of community. I remember it all, enough to write it down, so I know I do have something.

Acknowledgments

Major giant thank you to Leslie Miller for her belief in this project, her patient calmness, and her editing assistance, and to Rocco Kayiatos for his help and feedback and enthusiasm.

CONTRIBUTOR BIOGRAPHIES

Before settling down with husband and child in Chicago, **Maria Rivera** could be seen workin' the system in the trailer-trash suburbs of Detroit. From then until now, Maria has been polishing her ghetto-princess skills into an art form.

Colleen McKee is an M.F.A. student at the University of Missouri, St. Louis, and the winner of its graduate poetry award. Her essays, poetry, fiction and journalism have appeared in *Delmar, Bridges: A Journal for Jewish Feminists and Their Friends, Inter-Action Saint Louis, Ampersand,* and other publications. She has been an editor for *Natural Bridge, Confluence, Salamander,* and the St. Louis Art Museum. She teaches freshman composition and is the head librarian of the Bread and Roses Zine Library. Thanks to insurance ($263.35 of her $1,050 monthly salary), her health has greatly improved.

Lis Goldschmidt is a housepainter who lives in San Francisco. She also makes art and advocates for young people. Five is her favorite number.

Sailor Holladay is a twenty-three-year-old educator, student, bargain hunter, worker, actor, and poet. Sailor is committed to ending oppression on all levels and becoming more human every day.

Silas Howard (writer, director, producer, and musician) codirected her first feature with Harry Dodge, *By Hook or By Crook,* in 2001. It has garnered numerous awards at festivals including Outfest and South by Southwest. *By Hook or By Crook* has screened at Sundance and continues to air on the Sundance Channel. Silas was nominated, along with Harry Dodge, for a 2003 Rockefeller Media Award and was selected for the Nantucket Screenwriters Colony 2003. She has also performed nationally and internationally with her band, Tribe 8, the notorious punk/queercore band. Tribe 8 has been featured in *Rolling Stone, Village Voice, Interview, Ms.* magazine, *Billboard, Elle,* and the *Los Angeles Times.* A feature-length documentary about the band, *Rise Above,* received Best Documentary at the Frameline festival in San Francisco in 2003. Silas has produced and performed in numerous performance pieces around the Bay Area since 1990. She was also cofounder/owner of the legendary Red Dora's Bearded Lady Cafe and Truckstop, an acclaimed performing arts venue in San Francisco that won several awards for its spoken-word series. Silas can be reached at silas898@aol.com.

Meliza Bañales is a writer/spoken-word artist originally from Los Angeles. Her fiction, nonfiction, and poetry have been featured in *Laundry Pen, Lodestar Quarterly,* and *Revolutionary Voices,* to name a few. She is the 2002 Oakland Grand Slam Champion and the 2002 winner of the People Before Profits Poetry Prize. Her first collection of poems, *Say It With Your Whole Mouth,* came out in October of 2003 from Monkey Press. She lives in Oakland.

tatiana de la tierra (Villavicencio, Colombia, 1961) is an angry girl who rides horses in the sky and secretly wants to be a songwriter. She is the author of *For the Hard Ones: A Lesbian Phenomenology / Para las duras: Una fenomenología lesbiana* (Calaca / Chibcha Press), a bilingual celebration of lesbianism in poetic prose. She was cofounder and editor of the latina lesbian magazines *esto no tiene nombre* (1991–1994) and *conmoción* (1995–1996).

Shell Feijo is an Iowa graduate student by day, doing research to rid the world of classism, racism, and sexism. By night she is a soulful writer honestly pursuing a gift. Shell is the mom to two independent human spirits, four dogs, and three cats. Still in love after many crazy years with her partner, Sean, she lives in Iowa for now though the spirit of Northern California calls her home, just as the winters of a Canada she has never seen beckon her. Shell's first book, "Caterpillar in the Snow," is cocooning while searching for the wings to reach the public. Along with Sean, Kohl, Tam, Lissa, and a host of women friends keep her safe when the darkness falls.

Diane di Prima is a poet, teacher, psychic, playwright, healer, magician, anarchist, student of alchemy, and practitioner of Tibetan buddhism. She is the mother of five, grandmother of three, and a great-grandmother. A new edition of her *Revolutionary Letters* with twenty-three additional poems is being published by Last Gasp Press this fall, and Penguin is publishing *Opening to the Poem* (essays and exercises for beginning poets) next year. Her recent books include an autobiography, *Recollections of My Life as a Woman,* and her epic poem *Loba: Books I and II* (both from Penguin), and two chapbooks: *Towers Down* and *The Ones I Used to Laugh With.* She lives in San Francisco and teaches privately.

Liliana Hernández from Fairview, New Jersey, is a recent graduate from Smith College. Her previous work experience includes counseling of Dominican families affected by the Flight 587 crash in New York City, but most recently she worked in Kentucky as the Latina coordinator for the Democratic candidate's gubernatorial campaign. She hopes to travel the world, and is passionate about philosophy, activism, and working for social change. She focuses on the intersection of race, class, and ethnicity in her writing and spoken word.

Polyestra lives and writes in Montana, in a someday-to-be-heated log cabin beside the Yellowstone River, in a quasi-hermit-like state of pimp-like renovation and thrashing euphoria, taking care of business with the

Newt Gingrich–like assistance of a fluid-spewing disco-era brown-and-orange truck and a herding-crazed cow dog named Pinky, with her daughter and beautiful husband and musician Lenny America. She is a painter, a poet, the front woman for the band Polyestra, a filmmaker, and is at present active in no bullshit. You may have seen her perform somewhere in the USA in the last ten years. She has fifteen self-published books of poetry and art, some of which are available at powells.com, most of which are available at www.geocities.com/polyestraamerica.

Terri Griffith is a writer and artist who grew up in the Pacific Northwest. She currently lives in Chicago where she teaches writing and literature part-time at both Columbia College and The School of the Art Institute of Chicago. Her book reviews appear regularly in *BUST.*

Cassie Peterson moved from the depths of Wyoming to San Francisco almost five years ago. She now works as a sex educator at Good Vibrations *and* goes to school at New College of California, where she studies writing and literature. By the time this anthology comes out, she will be on the other side of the world, studying in Nepal and India. (And *yes* she will come back, and *no* she is not going to become a monk.) She occasionally does spontaneous and embarrassingly unrehearsed readings of her work and was last seen with a mike in her hands at Ladyfest Bay Area. This is her first officially published piece because she still has trouble believing that she can actually write. She loves to dance, watch dance, stalk dancers, and fraternize with potentially wealthy patrons who think she can actually write.

Eileen Myles is a poet and a novelist who teaches writing at University of California, San Diego. She's actually been in a state of shock for about a year since she now has enough money to live on for the first time ever. Her most recent books are *Skies,* and *on my way,* both poetry, and *Cool for You,* a novel. And she's working on a novel, "The Inferno," and an opera with the L.A. composer Michael Webster called "Hell" because it still is.

Terry Ryan, the sixth of Evelyn and Kelly Ryan's ten children, is the author of *The Prize Winner of Defiance, Ohio: How My Mother Raised 10 Kids on 25 Words or Less* (Simon & Schuster).

Dorothy Allison is the best-selling author of *Bastard Out of Carolina, Cavedweller,* and a memoir, *Two or Three Things I Know for Sure.* Born in Greenville, South Carolina, she currently lives with her partner and her son in Northern California.

Tara Hardy is the working-class femme dyke Poet Populist (elected by the people) of Seattle. She is the director of Bent Writing Institute, a school for queer writers in Seattle. She believes art is a tool for social change. Her poems, essays, and novel-in-progress explore gender, sexuality, social class, and race. Tara grew up in Michigan, then lived in Chicago and Philadelphia, before landing in Seattle. She recently finished her M.F.A. in fiction from Vermont College. You can email her at wordyfemme@hotmail.com to find out more about Bent, or to discuss her favorite topic: small dogs.

Wendy Thompson was born in Oakland, California, in 1981 and moved to the suburban city of Freemont at the age of fifteen. Her literary work has appeared in the anthologies *Restoried Selves* and *Yell-Oh Girls,* as well as online at generationrice.com. She received her B.A. in Asian American Studies from the University of California, Riverside and is currently a doctoral student at the University of Maryland, College Park. Donations are always appreciated.

Daisy Hernández is the coeditor with Bushra Rehman of *Colonize This! Young Women of Color on Today's Feminism* (Seal Press). She has written a column for *Ms.* magazine, reported for the *New York Times,* and is now very proud to be in the same anthology as her sister, Liliana. When Daisy is not busy being a dutiful daughter and analyzing the impact of NAFTA on her parents' lives, she is a hardcore, fuck-or-fight, gets-her-nails-done Jersey femme living in San Francisco. Daisy is a Gemini.

Siobhan Brooks was born and raised in San Francisco and now lives in New York, where she is studying sociology at New School University. She was a union organizer at the Lusty Lady Theater, and has been published in *Colonize This! Young Women of Color on Today's Feminism* (Seal Press), *Hastings Women's Law Journal, Z* Magazine, and *Feminism and Anti-Racism.* She is an adjunct professor of sociology and women's studies at Lehman College.

Tina Fakhrid-Deen works in the nonprofit sector and is the Chicago chapter coordinator for COLAGE (Children of Lesbians and Gays Everywhere). She is a writer who also loves to perform and direct plays. She resides in Chicago with her beautiful husband, Jashed, and their toddler, Khari Yasmeen. Tina is currently working on a collection of essays about African-American children with LGBT parents and a book about "How to Unlock Dreadlocked Hair."

Bee Lavender is the coeditor of two books: *Breeder* (Seal Press) and the forthcoming anthology "Mamaphonic" (Soft Skull). Bee is the publisher of the online edition of *Hip Mama* and the founder of Girl-Mom.com, an advocacy and community resource site for teen parents. Bee is also the author of the zine series *A Beautiful Final Tribute.* She is currently writing a book about radical education and youth liberation.

Joy Castro is Associate Professor of English at Wabash College. Adopted at birth by a family of Jehovah's Witnesses, she ran away at fourteen. Her fiction and essays have appeared in *Mid-American Review, Chelsea, North American Review, Quarterly West, Puerto del Sol, Indianapolis Monthly, Cream City Review,* and other journals, and in anthologies. Her scholarly work focuses on experimental, leftist women writers, and her current project is a critical study of modernist Margery Latimer (1899–1932). She lives with her husband and son in Indiana.

Ida Dewey Acton is a writer, playwright, visual artist, and cosmetology student, and at the moment she is still managing to eke out a living in San

Francisco. She recently wrote, directed, produced, and acted in her play *Hair-trigger Heart,* which sold out all shows at Theatre Spanganga in June 2003. Ida is currently working on her novel, "The Sad and Terrible Ballad of Haskal J." Lonesome. She is a touring and recording veteran of Sister Spit and has performed at the National Queer Arts Festival, The Harvey Milk Readers and Writers Conference, and the Michigan Womyn's Music Festival among other places. She loves humid, southern summers; clean, crisp pillowcases; and her dogs.

Frances Varian is a writer and performer who lives in Seattle, Washington. For the past five years she has worked as a women's/queer healthcare advocate. She wants to thank Puppy, whose insistent nagging is responsible for this essay.

Nikki Levine is a twenty-three-year-old Jersey girl who did time in Washington, D.C., during the rise of the machines. She's femme, a high-school dropout, a self-taught UNIX engineer, and a wannabe millionaire. Nikki likes to drive, write, eat, and convert Kirk Hammett guitar solos to keyboard. She's a Taurus with Leo rising, Sagittarius moon.

Ricky Lee is a native midwesterner residing in San Francisco. She is a mover of things heavy and a washer of things disgusting. She is a poet, painter, a bassist for the band Ghost Cat, and occasionally she raps under the MC name The Real McKnight. She also runs TroubleMaker Productions company, which, when it has time, curates art shows featuring working-class artists, shoots pornos that will never be seen by the general public, and has released such noteworthy shorts as *Reservoir Dykes,* as well as the brand-new, red-hot, sizzling rap video "Hella Ho's." She is currently living off unemployment and will be in need of a new job by the time this book is published—if you want to give her money or a job please contact ghostcatupyours@hotmail.com.

Hadassah M. Hill is a queer, femme, expat American who has been writing and doing spoken-word performance for about ten years. She has a fashion and costume design company, Dirty Boots Design, and loves rock music, vintage and subversive literature. She lives in Toronto.

Leah Lakshmi Piepzna-Samarasinha is a fierce, fearless queer Sri Lankan writer, spoken word artist, activist, and survivor dreaming of a decolonized world and working to make it happen in her lifetime. She was born and raised in Worcester, a.k.a. Wormtown/Wartown, Massachusetts, matured in Brooklyn, and currently squats in Toronto. Her work has appeared in the anthologies *Colonize This! Young Women of Color on Today's Feminism* (Seal Press), *Dangerous Families: Queers Surviving Sexual Abuse* (Harrington Park Press), the Lambda-nominated *Brazen Femmes: Queering Femininity* (Arsenal Pulp), *Geeks, Misfits and Outlaws* (McGilligan), *Bent on Writing* (Women's Press), *Fireweed, big boots, Bamboo Girl, Anything That Moves,* and her zines *Letters from the War Years* and *Breedlove.* She has performed her work at many conferences, slam venues, protests, and universities, including appearances at Yale University, Oberlin College, the 2003 API Spoken Word Summit, SALAAM's international queer Muslim conference, the Color of Violence 2 Conference, and the Nuyorican Poet's Cafe. She is currently finishing her first book, "Consensual Genocide," teaching writing to queer and trans kids, and running browngirlworld, a queer, of color, spoken word/beatz night in Toronto.

Shawna Kenney is the author of the award-winning memoir, *I Was a Teenage Dominatrix.* She has written for *Juxtapoz, Transworld Skateboarding, Slap, Tease, Alternative Press, SG, The Underground Guide to Los Angeles, While You Were Sleeping, Herbivore Magazine,* Epitaph Records, and herself.

ABOUT THE EDITOR

Michelle Tea is the author of two novels, *The Passionate Mistakes and Intricate Corruption of One Girl in America* (Semiotext(e)) and the Lambda Literary Award–winning *Valencia* (Seal Press), and an award-nominated memoir, *The Chelsea Whistle*. Her work has appeared in various anthologies and publications. Forthcoming in 2004 are a collection of Tea's poetry titled *The Beautiful* (Manic D Press); collected edgy, first-person narratives, coedited with Clint Catalyst, titled *Pills, Thrills, Chills and Heartache* (Alyson Publications); and *Best Lesbian Erotica 2004*, which she guest-edited for Cleis Press. She is also at work on an illustrated novel, "Rent Girl," with artist Laurenn McCubbin. Tea lives in San Francisco.

Selected Titles from Seal Press

The Chelsea Whistle by Michelle Tea. $14.95, 1-58005-073-5. In this gritty, confessional memoir, Michelle Tea takes the reader back to the city of her childhood: Chelsea, Massachusetts—Boston's ugly, scrappy little sister and a place where time and hope are spent on things not getting any worse.

Valencia by Michelle Tea. $13.00, 1-58005-035-2. This is the fast-paced account of one girl's search for love and high times in a place where everything matters and nothing matters, and all tragedies and ecstasies weigh equally. By turns poetic and frantic, *Valencia* is an edgy, visceral ride through the queer girl underworld of the Mission district of San Francisco.

Cunt: A Declaration of Independence by Inga Muscio. $14.95, 1-58005-075-1. An ancient title of respect for women, "cunt" long ago veered off the path of honor and now careens toward the heart of every woman as an expletive. Muscio traces this winding road, giving women both the motivation and the tools to claim "cunt" as a positive and powerful force in the lives of all women.

Listen Up: Voices from the Next Feminist Generation edited by Barbara Findlen. $16.95, 1-58005-054-9. A revised and expanded edition of the Seal Press classic, featuring the voices of a new generation of women expressing the vibrancy and vitality of today's feminist movement.

Colonize This! Young Women of Color on Today's Feminism edited by Daisy Hernández and Bushra Rehman. $16.95, 1-58005-067-0. It has been decades since women of color first turned feminism upside down. Now a new generation of brilliant, outspoken women of color is speaking to the concerns of a new feminism, and their place in it.

Sometimes Rhythm, Sometimes Blues: Young African Americans on Love, Relationships, Sex, and the Search for Mr. Right edited by Taigi Smith. $15.95, 1-58005-096-4. A tell-it-like-it-is look at black women's tumultuous search for love and partnership in their community.

Seal Press publishes many books of fiction and nonfiction by women writers. Please visit our Web site at **www.sealpress.com**.